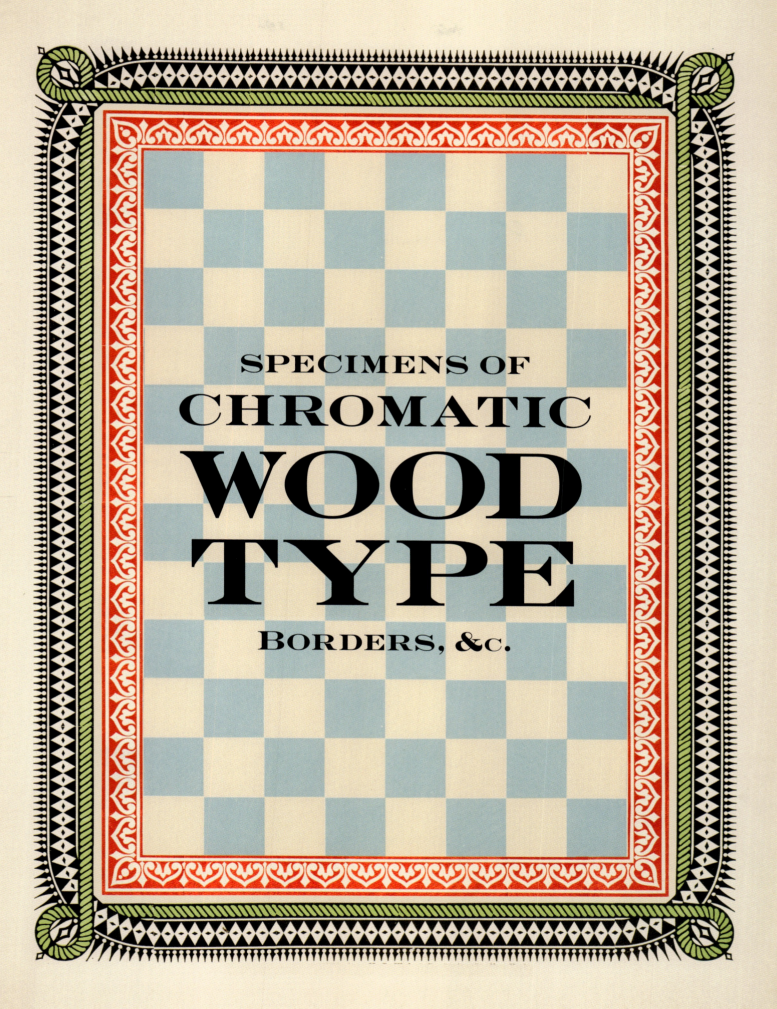

SPECIMENS OF
CHROMATIC
WOOD
TYPE
BORDERS, &c.

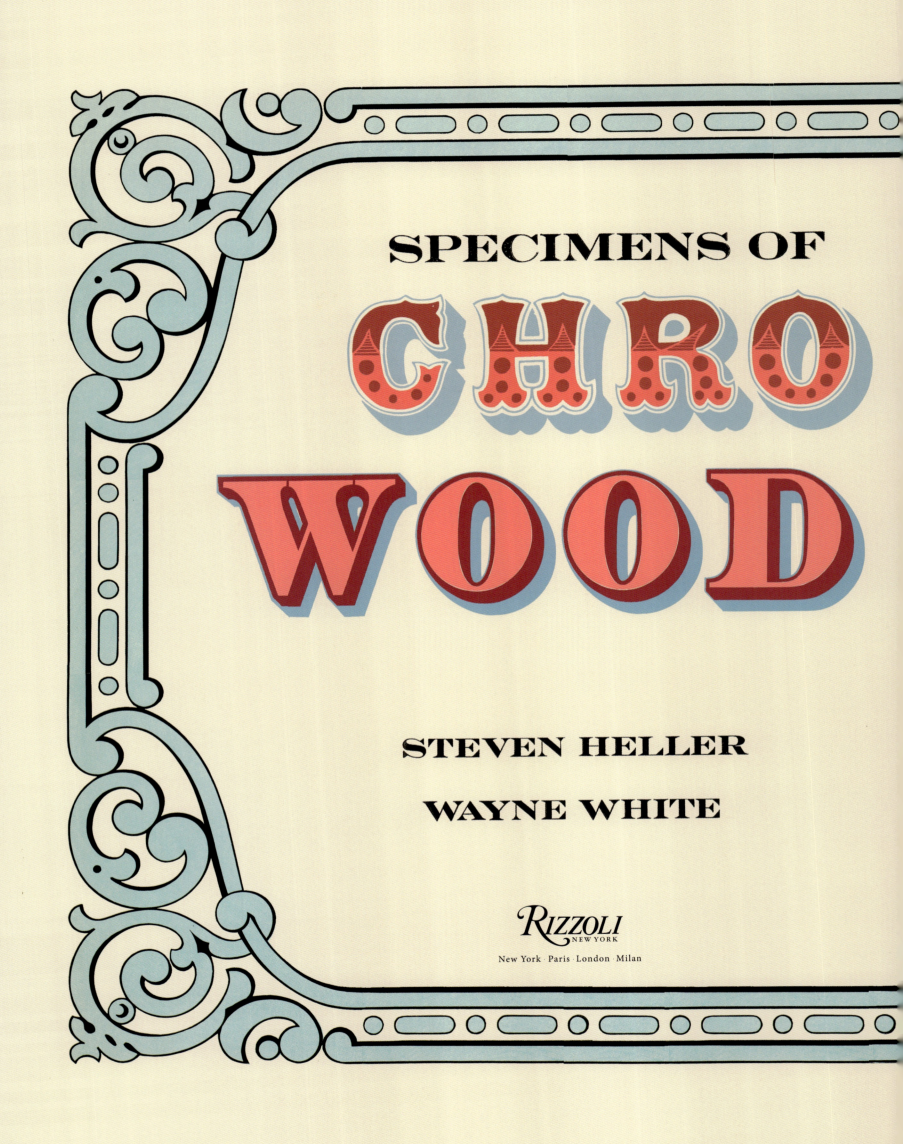

SPECIMENS OF
CHRO WOOD

STEVEN HELLER
WAYNE WHITE

RIZZOLI
NEW YORK
New York · Paris · London · Milan

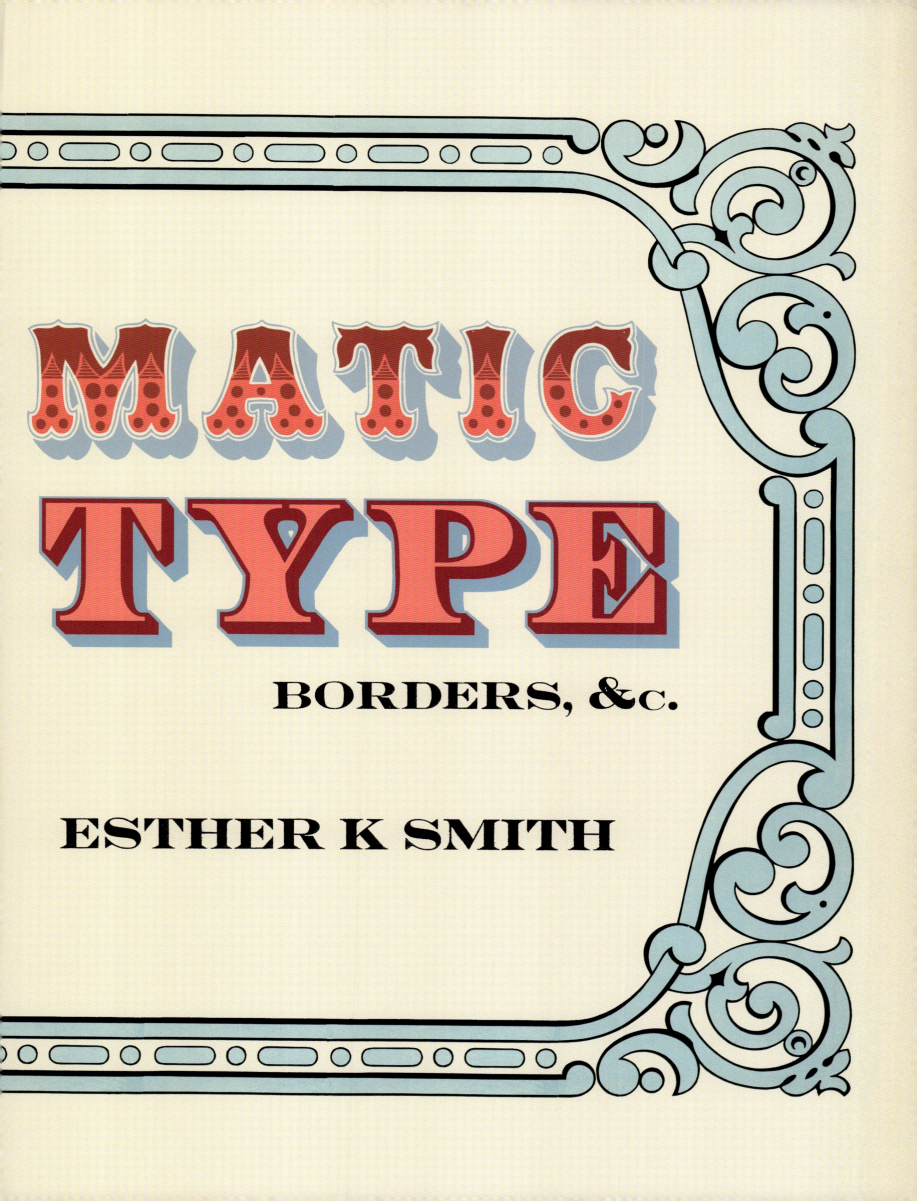

MATIC TYPE

BORDERS, &c.

ESTHER K SMITH

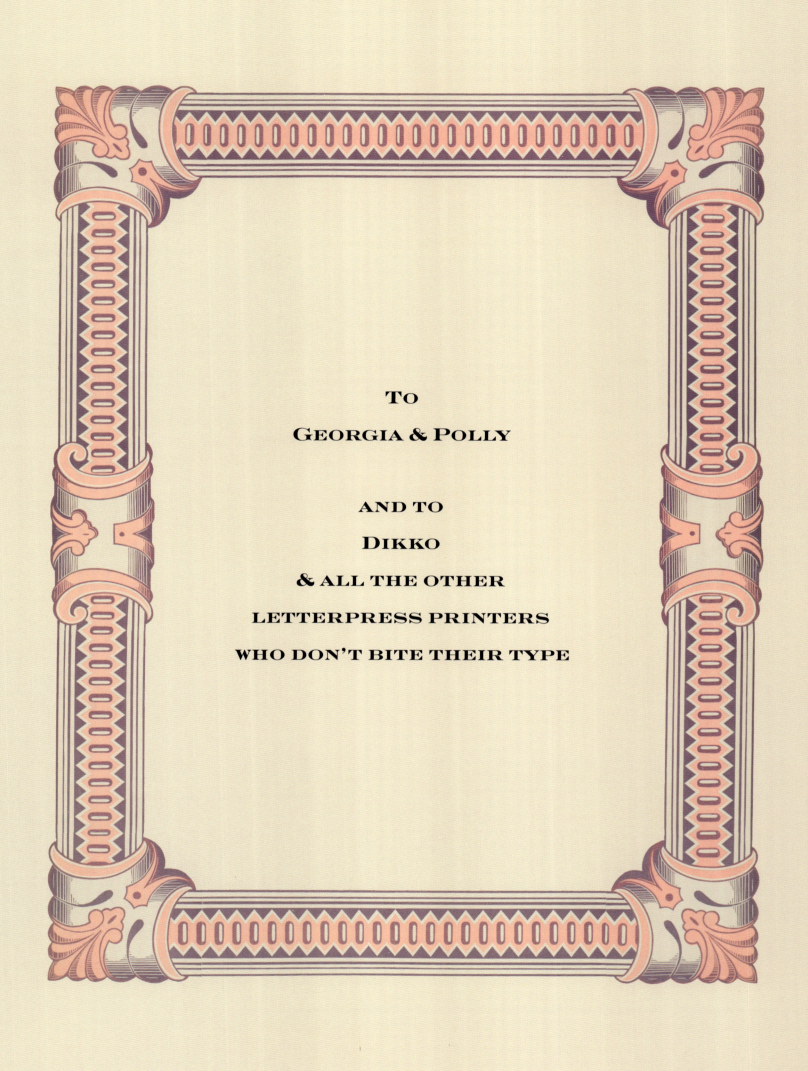

To

GEORGIA & POLLY

AND TO

DIKKO

& ALL THE OTHER

LETTERPRESS PRINTERS

WHO DON'T BITE THEIR TYPE

CONTENTS

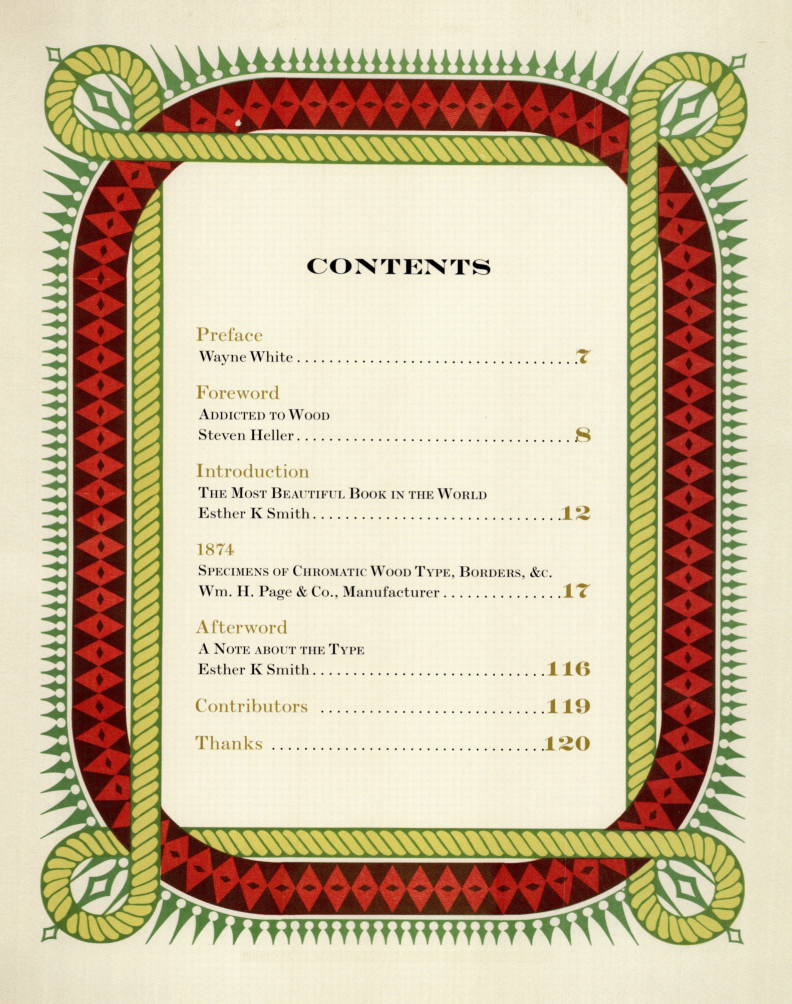

First published in the United States of America in 2017
by Rizzoli International Publications, Inc.
300 Park Avenue South
New York, NY 10010
www.rizzoliusa.com

2017 2018 2019 2020 2021 / 10 9 8 7 6 5 4 3 2 1

Distributed in the U.S. trade by Random House, New York

Cover & book design: Esther K Smith, Purgatory Pie Press
Handset type: Dikko Faust
Design production: Alice Curiel, Jennifer King
Design consultant: Amy Sly
Photo retouching: Aaron Schoenfelder

Printed in China

ISBN-13: 978-0-8478-5868-2
Library of Congress Catalog Control Number: 2016953538

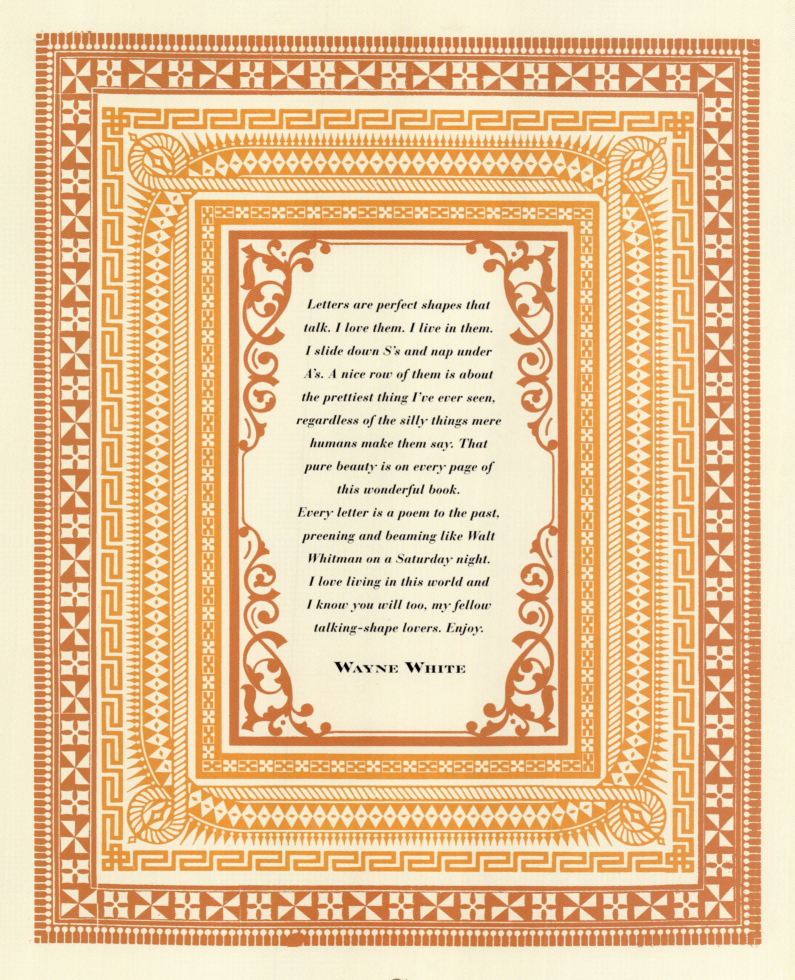

Letters are perfect shapes that talk. I love them. I live in them. I slide down S's and nap under A's. A nice row of them is about the prettiest thing I've ever seen, regardless of the silly things mere humans make them say. That pure beauty is on every page of this wonderful book.

Every letter is a poem to the past, preening and beaming like Walt Whitman on a Saturday night. I love living in this world and I know you will too, my fellow talking-shape lovers. Enjoy.

WAYNE WHITE

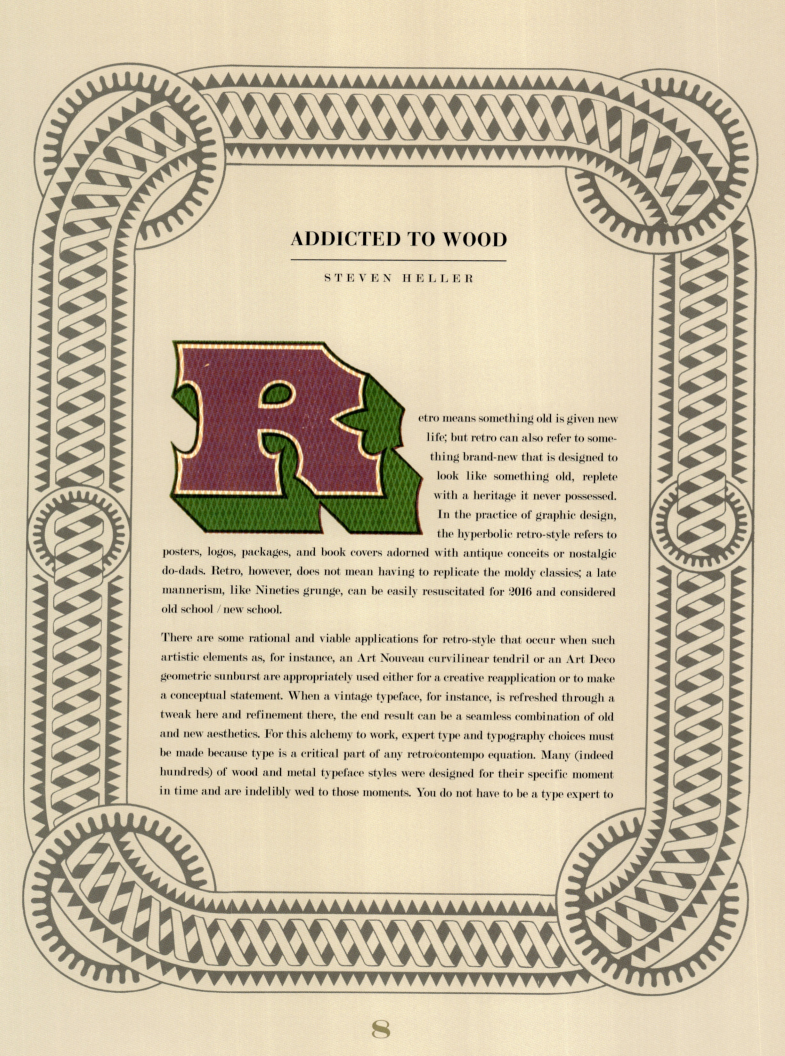

ADDICTED TO WOOD

S T E V E N   H E L L E R

Retro means something old is given new life; but retro can also refer to something brand-new that is designed to look like something old, replete with a heritage it never possessed. In the practice of graphic design, the hyperbolic retro-style refers to posters, logos, packages, and book covers adorned with antique conceits or nostalgic do-dads. Retro, however, does not mean having to replicate the moldy classics; a late mannerism, like Nineties grunge, can be easily resuscitated for 2016 and considered old school / new school.

There are some rational and viable applications for retro-style that occur when such artistic elements as, for instance, an Art Nouveau curvilinear tendril or an Art Deco geometric sunburst are appropriately used either for a creative reapplication or to make a conceptual statement. When a vintage typeface, for instance, is refreshed through a tweak here and refinement there, the end result can be a seamless combination of old and new aesthetics. For this alchemy to work, expert type and typography choices must be made because type is a critical part of any retro/contempo equation. Many (indeed hundreds) of wood and metal typeface styles were designed for their specific moment in time and are indelibly wed to those moments. You do not have to be a type expert to

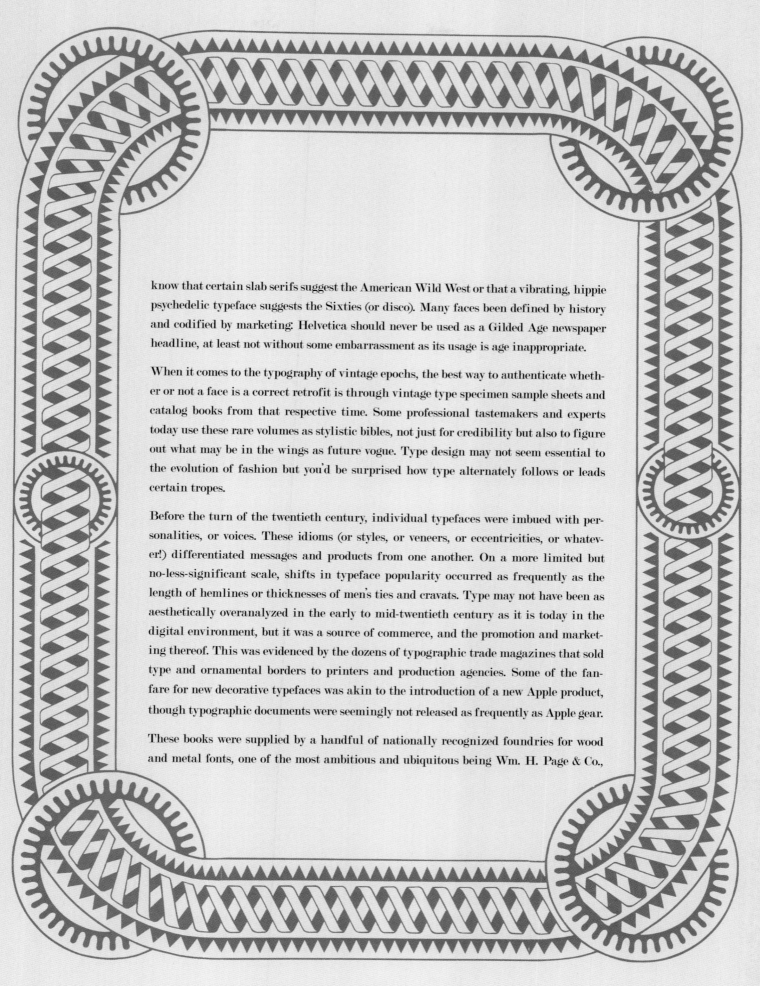

know that certain slab serifs suggest the American Wild West or that a vibrating, hippie psychedelic typeface suggests the Sixties (or disco). Many faces been defined by history and codified by marketing: Helvetica should never be used as a Gilded Age newspaper headline, at least not without some embarrassment as its usage is age inappropriate.

When it comes to the typography of vintage epochs, the best way to authenticate whether or not a face is a correct retrofit is through vintage type specimen sample sheets and catalog books from that respective time. Some professional tastemakers and experts today use these rare volumes as stylistic bibles, not just for credibility but also to figure out what may be in the wings as future vogue. Type design may not seem essential to the evolution of fashion but you'd be surprised how type alternately follows or leads certain tropes.

Before the turn of the twentieth century, individual typefaces were imbued with personalities, or voices. These idioms (or styles, or veneers, or eccentricities, or whatever!) differentiated messages and products from one another. On a more limited but no-less-significant scale, shifts in typeface popularity occurred as frequently as the length of hemlines or thicknesses of men's ties and cravats. Type may not have been as aesthetically overanalyzed in the early to mid-twentieth century as it is today in the digital environment, but it was a source of commerce, and the promotion and marketing thereof. This was evidenced by the dozens of typographic trade magazines that sold type and ornamental borders to printers and production agencies. Some of the fanfare for new decorative typefaces was akin to the introduction of a new Apple product, though typographic documents were seemingly not released as frequently as Apple gear.

These books were supplied by a handful of nationally recognized foundries for wood and metal fonts, one of the most ambitious and ubiquitous being Wm. H. Page & Co.,

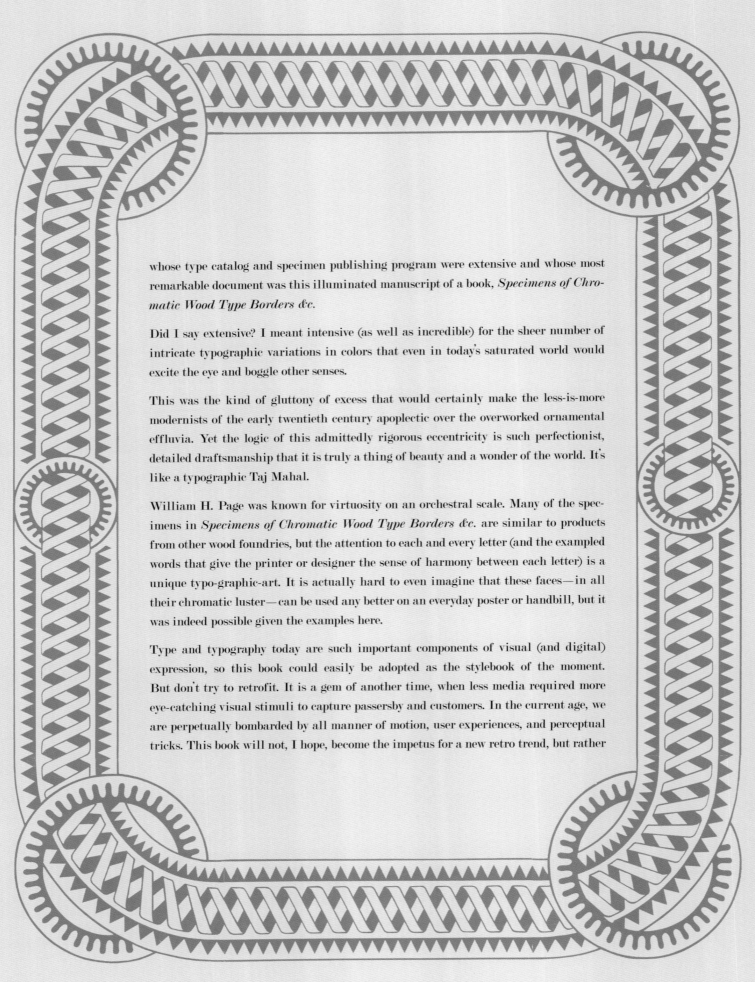

whose type catalog and specimen publishing program were extensive and whose most remarkable document was this illuminated manuscript of a book, *Specimens of Chromatic Wood Type Borders &c.*

Did I say extensive? I meant intensive (as well as incredible) for the sheer number of intricate typographic variations in colors that even in today's saturated world would excite the eye and boggle other senses.

This was the kind of gluttony of excess that would certainly make the less-is-more modernists of the early twentieth century apoplectic over the overworked ornamental effluvia. Yet the logic of this admittedly rigorous eccentricity is such perfectionist, detailed draftsmanship that it is truly a thing of beauty and a wonder of the world. It's like a typographic Taj Mahal.

William H. Page was known for virtuosity on an orchestral scale. Many of the specimens in *Specimens of Chromatic Wood Type Borders &c.* are similar to products from other wood foundries, but the attention to each and every letter (and the exampled words that give the printer or designer the sense of harmony between each letter) is a unique typo-graphic-art. It is actually hard to even imagine that these faces—in all their chromatic luster—can be used any better on an everyday poster or handbill, but it was indeed possible given the examples here.

Type and typography today are such important components of visual (and digital) expression, so this book could easily be adopted as the stylebook of the moment. But don't try to retrofit. It is a gem of another time, when less media required more eye-catching visual stimuli to capture passersby and customers. In the current age, we are perpetually bombarded by all manner of motion, user experiences, and perceptual tricks. This book will not, I hope, become the impetus for a new retro trend, but rather

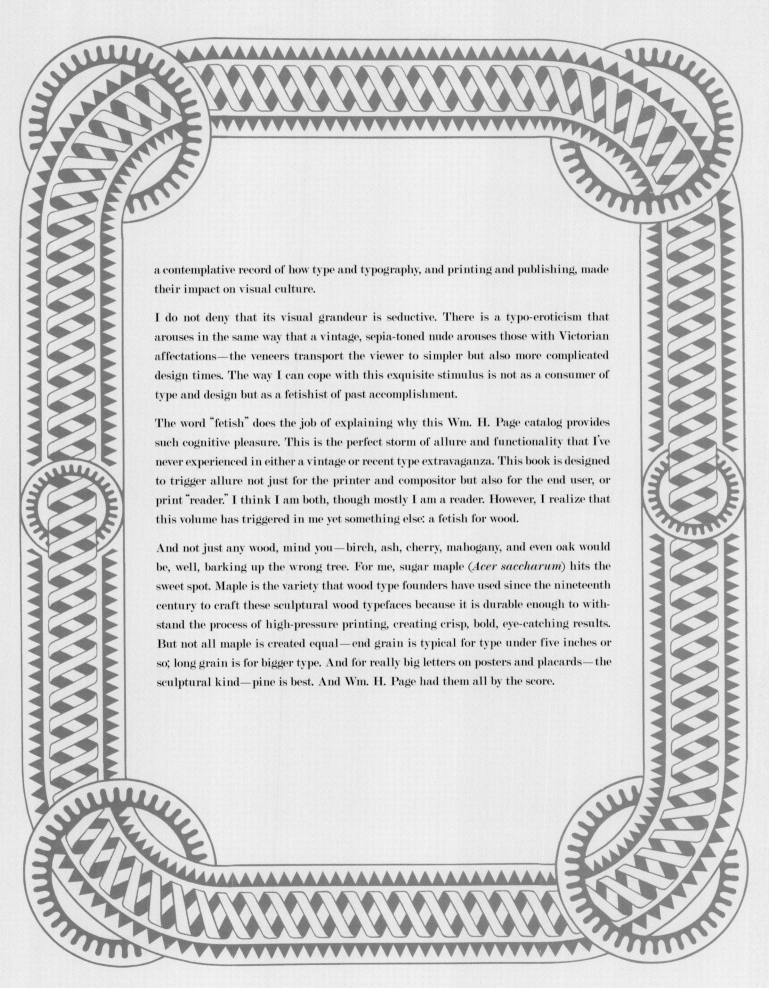

a contemplative record of how type and typography, and printing and publishing, made their impact on visual culture.

I do not deny that its visual grandeur is seductive. There is a typo-eroticism that arouses in the same way that a vintage, sepia-toned nude arouses those with Victorian affectations—the veneers transport the viewer to simpler but also more complicated design times. The way I can cope with this exquisite stimulus is not as a consumer of type and design but as a fetishist of past accomplishment.

The word "fetish" does the job of explaining why this Wm. H. Page catalog provides such cognitive pleasure. This is the perfect storm of allure and functionality that I've never experienced in either a vintage or recent type extravaganza. This book is designed to trigger allure not just for the printer and compositor but also for the end user, or print "reader." I think I am both, though mostly I am a reader. However, I realize that this volume has triggered in me yet something else: a fetish for wood.

And not just any wood, mind you—birch, ash, cherry, mahogany, and even oak would be, well, barking up the wrong tree. For me, sugar maple (*Acer saccharum*) hits the sweet spot. Maple is the variety that wood type founders have used since the nineteenth century to craft these sculptural wood typefaces because it is durable enough to withstand the process of high-pressure printing, creating crisp, bold, eye-catching results. But not all maple is created equal—end grain is typical for type under five inches or so; long grain is for bigger type. And for really big letters on posters and placards—the sculptural kind—pine is best. And Wm. H. Page had them all by the score.

THE MOST BEAUTIFUL BOOK IN THE WORLD

ESTHER K SMITH

first saw *Specimens of Chromatic Wood Type, Borders &c.* at The Newberry Library in 2013. I had first heard of it in 1998, when Dikko Faust walked in, stunned, awed, and ecstatic, plopped into a chair, breathless, and said, "I have just seen the most beautiful book in the world!" I did not pay much attention, I was busy with something. I did not rush up to see it. But fifteen years later, when I opened The Newberry's copy of this book, I remembered.

Dikko and I make limited editions and artist books at Purgatory Pie Press in New York City. We collaborate. Dikko hand sets antique wood and metal type and prints on a vintage Vandercook 4 letterpress. I think up concepts, play with book structures, and stitch our books. For some projects we bring in other writers or artists. Helpers and colleagues participate when we need them. Dikko is the founder, typographer, printer. Someone told me I am the artistic director. That means I do everything else.

Dikko also teaches, and he had been at the New York Public Library with his City College typography students when rare books librarian Virginia Bartow pulled a large, thin volume from a cart and said, "Dikko, you're gonna like this." It was too tall for their standard shelves. The book had just been put somewhere when Virginia found it.

When I first saw *Chromatic Wood Type* at The Newberry, we were on our way to speak at a conference at Hamilton Wood Type Museum. We had a behind-the-scenes tour that ended in a study room. Librarians Jill Gage and Paul Gehl had pulled some rare wood type books, and we were looking at them, snapping photos. They were all lovely.

And then I opened this fourteen-by-eighteen-inch slender volume with a simple dark green cover: Wm. H. Page & Co.'s 1874 *Specimens of Chromatic Wood Type, Borders &c.* It took up most of the table. I said something. And Dikko said, "Wait for it."

And I was turning pages, reading the price list, wishing I could buy that type for those prices, but also thinking, it was never cheap. And I turned more pages—and the black-and-white letter forms were so interesting. And Dikko said, "Keep going." And then

OH MY GOD. I got to one of the full-color pages and I wanted that book. And I kept turning the pages. And I fell in love.

I wanted the book. But it was rare. Even if I could find one, it would cost a fortune. But I wanted to show it to my friends. I wanted to show it to my students. And as I turned the pages, I thought, "I could reprint this book so I can have one." I wanted to show it to everyone, I wanted to show it to YOU. For the color alone. For its crazy found poetry. And of course for the typography—that ultimate wood type. For the experience and the inspiration. Even if it was not fascinating and historical, this catalog is a timeless treasure, like some wonderful painting or sculpture or opera. Like architecture. Like jazz.

How rare is it? I have seen two copies at the New York Public Library. I saw that copy at The Newberry—and went back to see it again. I have been working with Columbia University's three copies in their marvelous graphic design collection. They are similar but have some slight differences. Several pages show up in alternate colors. One 1876 copy has a paste-in discount price sheet. There are copies at the Historical Society in Connecticut where Page had his factory, and Harvard and Rochester Institute of Technology, and The Huntington rare books library in Pasadena, California, along with their Gutenberg Bible. The Metropolitan Museum lists a copy in their catalog—but we have not been able to see it yet.

Page printed one thousand—where did they all go? Maybe you will find one.

Everyone I know in wood type said I should talk to David Shields. (Read his *Wood Type Research* blog!) So I called David to ask him what he thought was the current technological invention equivalent to Page's wood type. I was thinking something like 3-D printing. His answer surprised me. He said it was the Internet. Or iPhones. We have posters today, but David said that in 1874 people got their news of the world from posters when they walked to work—even more than from newspapers, which they would have had to buy and to read. Artisans painted signs on sides of barns and buildings—but the development of large wood type meant that multiples of the same poster could be printed and pasted up. Their message was inescapable.

At that time, people handset and letterpress-printed all words and texts from pieces of movable metal and wood type. The largest standard metal type is around an inch—though it can go up to two inches. Wood type is much, much bigger.

In the original fourteen-by-eighteen-inch *Chromatic Wood Type* some words are twelve inches tall. The word "SIN" in huge letters made me think of revival meeting posters. The book's order forms include type up to 120 lines, about twenty inches tall. And printers could special order larger sizes. At Purgatory Pie Press, we have a wooden "&"

that is too big for our press. And we have seen wood type letters taller than a man. Rob Roy Kelly in *American Wood Type* wrote that Wm. H. Page & Co.'s largest type was more than ten feet tall and seven feet wide. Each letter took nine tiled wood blocks. That is what people saw instead of texting when they walked to work in those days before Internet, cell phones, computers, television, radio, or even recorded music.

William H. Page was born in 1829—right after wood type was invented. He apprenticed with a printer, worked for newspapers, and in 1855 he got a job making wood type for J. G. Cooley. After a year, seeing how he could improve precision, Page and a partner, Bassett, bought the failed wood type factory H. & J. Bill & Co. When Bassett left, a machinist named Mowry became Page's next partner, and the "Co." in Wm. H. Page & Co. In 1869, they bought out Cooley, Page's old employer. In a letter when he was selling his company, Page wrote:

> *We bought out the Cooley Wood Type Works…paid him $30,000. His patterns were only duplicates of ours so we burned them for fire wood. We did this to get him out of the way. It paid us well enough.*

Page hired women during the Civil War and they continued to work for him after the men returned home. *Great Industries of the United States* (1872) wrote, "This establishment gives employment to a large number of hands, a goodly portion of whom are females, who exhibit great skill in the manipulation of the deft and delicate machinery."

Page's cost for printing *Chromatic Wood Type* in 1874 was $10,000 for one thousand copies (Rob Roy Kelly, *American Wood Type*). Ten dollars per book was more than most workers made in a week then. The book was for marketing to the trade only, distributed to agents—who would call on the finest printers all over the world to sell the type. Note the warning on many pages:

DO NOT CUT THIS BOOK.

Had it been sold to the public, Page's cost would have quadrupled—doubled for wholesale and doubled again—or even increased ten-fold for retail. Adjusted for inflation, the printing would have cost $250 per book, and they would have retailed for $1,000 to $2,500 each.

Besides advertising Page's wood type, *Chromatic Wood Type* promoted Wade's ink—which was on Ann Street in New York City, a few blocks from where Purgatory Pie Press is now. Wade moved his ink factory to 117 Fulton Street a few years later and then 25 Reade Street—even closer to our studio. (If only we could go to Wade's for our letterpress inks now!) Wade's inks were lightfast, high quality, and "good to the bottom of the can!" The U.S. Bureau of Engraving and Printing bought their ink from Wade.

The availability of crazy ink colors may have driven this whole project. Coal tar aniline dyes and artificial colors had just been developed by an eighteen-year-old London chemist named William Perkin. Trying to invent artificial quinine to treat malaria, Perkin stained a piece of silk purple—and it would not wash out. He named his color mauve. Now you can buy paint, crayons, inks in all colors at a store—or, as our art stores are going out-of-business, order online. But until the industrial revolution, people had to find colors, dig them, mine them, grow them, or for the brightest reds, crush cochineal beetles. Before Perkin's mauve, purple dye came from the glandular mucus of particular mollusks.

Page published *Chromatic Wood Type* before halftone printing, which was invented a few years later for photographic reproduction. So now when pink is a halftone dot tint of red, in 1874 pink was a separate color. But, by layering two transparent inks, you could get a third color. That was the revolution of chromatic wood type, printed with transparent inks.

Take a close look at page 17, *Chromatic Wood Type*'s original title page, it has nine colors. It's not my favorite (that may be page 63, RUSTIC BRIDE MUN). In 1874, the printer had to feed that piece of paper through the press nine times. Their registration was exquisite. But take a good look. There is a typo—can you find it? If not, the answer is on page 118. When they made the 1876 edition of this book, Page had moved his factory to a new address, and changed the name to The Wm. H. Page Wood Type Co. when his partner Mowry retired. The very pretty title page of that edition has just two colors: black and gray.

On January 4, 1891, James Hamilton of Two Rivers, Wisconsin (now the Wood Type Museum) bought The Wm. H. Page Wood Type Co. William Page sold out to finance his new venture: steam heat. He patented radiators. If you are warm in the winter, you can thank him for that as well for his typography.

When we were setting up Purgatory Pie Press, we had to find, rescue, and/or buy vintage printing equipment and used metal and wood type. Now Virgin Wood Type and Moore Wood Type have begun manufacturing new wood type. I am thrilled that the letterpress revival includes these delightful people, who are both reproducing Wm. H. Page typefaces. Dikko's student Han Ju Cho did a Purgatory Pie Press internship for credit after acing his letterpress course at School of Visual Arts. Han Ju designed a wood typeface, Guaviq, and laser-cut it on end-grain maple. I feel honored to witness the resurrection of this beautiful lost type, this craft, this art.

I would rather own this book than the Gutenberg Bible.

When I said that, my editor told me to put it in my introduction.

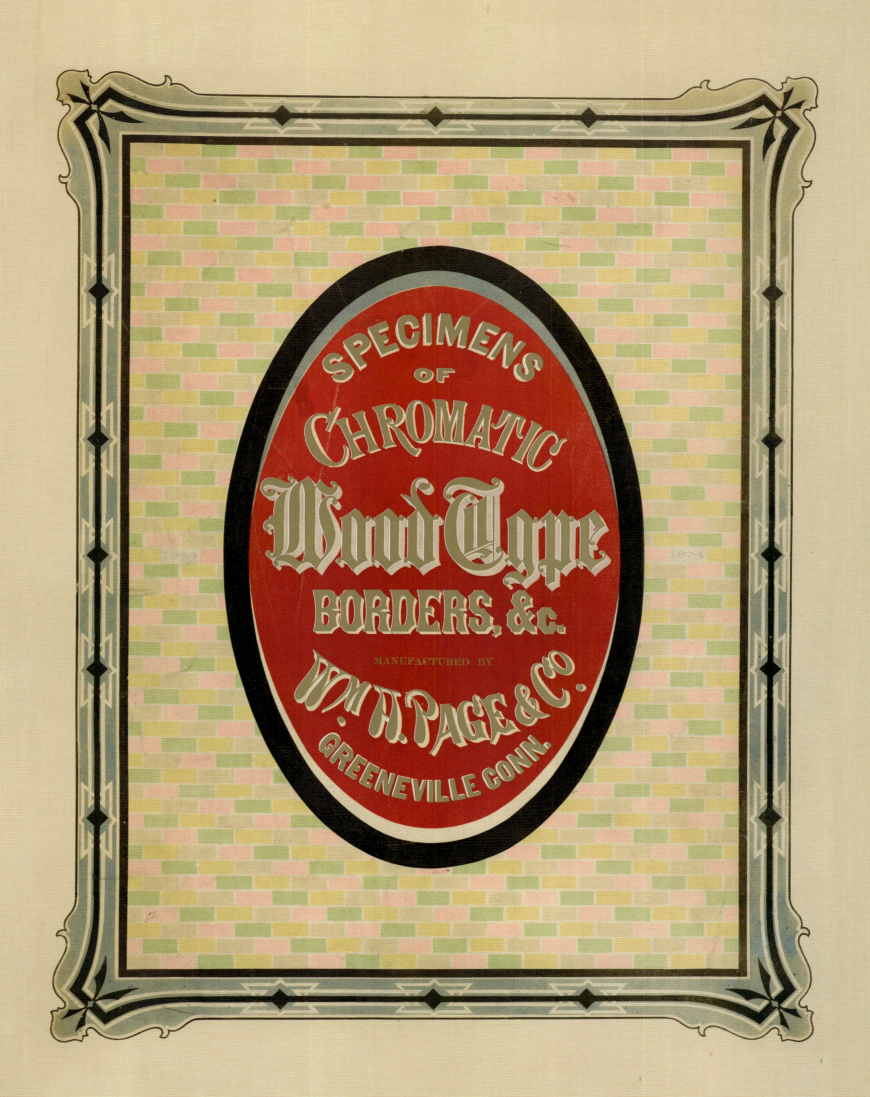

SPECIMENS
OF
CHROMATIC
Wood Type
BORDERS, &c.
MANUFACTURED BY
Wm. H. PAGE & CO.
GREENEVILLE CONN.

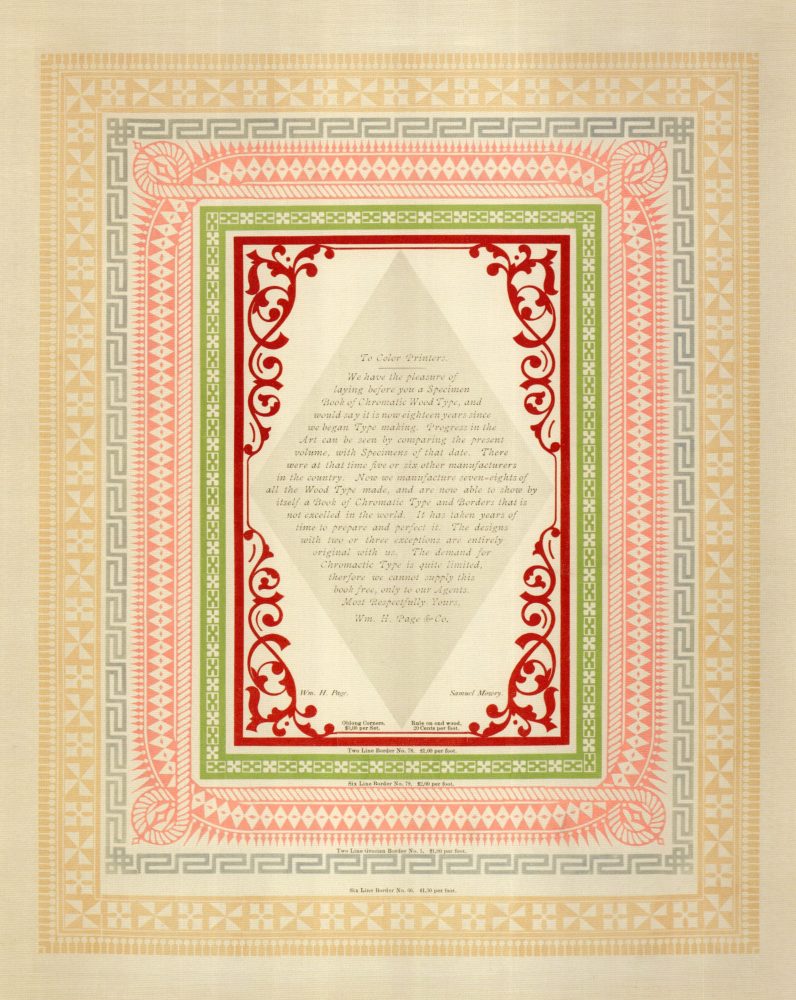

To Color Printers.

We have the pleasure of laying before you a Specimen Book of Chromatic Wood Type, and would say it is now eighteen years since we began Type making. Progress in the Art can be seen by comparing the present volume, with Specimens of that date. There were at that time five or six other manufacturers in the country. Now we manufacture seven-eighths of all the Wood Type made, and are now able to show by itself a Book of Chromatic Type and Borders that is not excelled in the world. It has taken years of time to prepare and perfect it. The designs with two or three exceptions are entirely original with us. The demand for Chromactic Type is quite limited, therfore we cannot supply this book free, only to our Agents.

Most Respectfully Yours,

Wm. H. Page & Co.

Wm. H. Page.   Samuel Mowry.

Oblong Corners.   Rule on end wood,
$3.00 per Set.   20 Cents per foot.

Two Line Border No. 78. $1.00 per foot.

Six Line Border No. 79. $2.00 per foot.

Two Line Grecian Border No. 1. $1.00 per foot.

Six Line Border No. 66. $1.50 per foot.

Price List of Chromatic Wood Type, Borders &c.

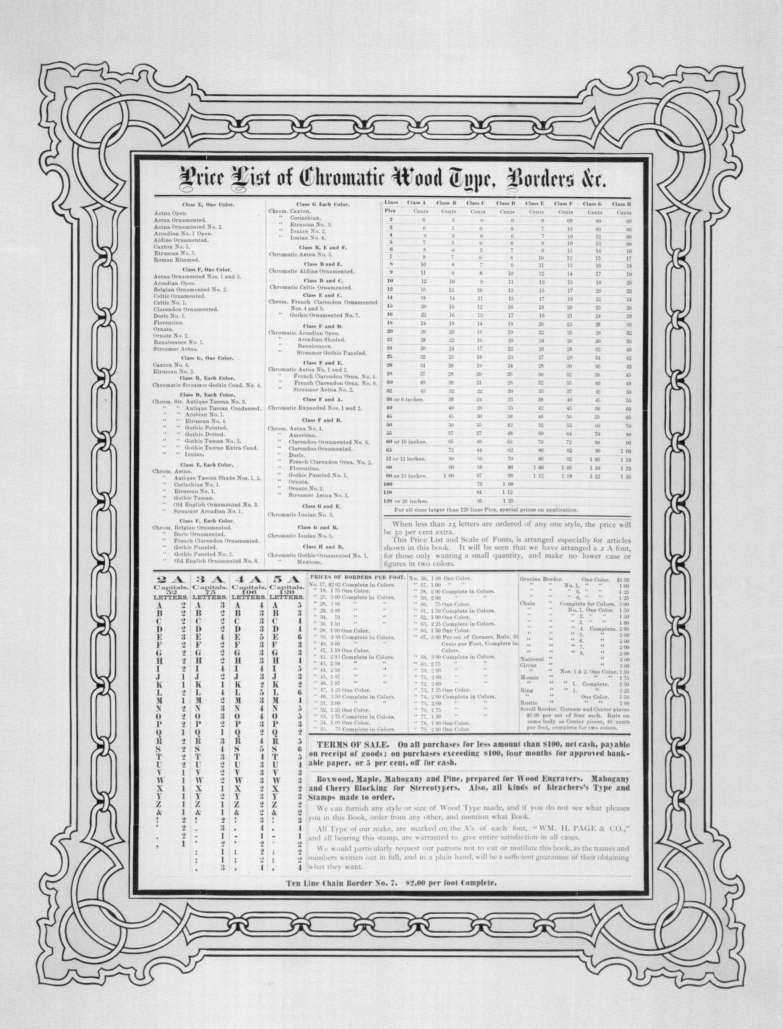

Class E, One Color.
Aetna Open.
Aetna Ornamented.
Aetna Ornamented No. 2.
Arcadian No. 1 Open.
Aldine Ornamented.
Caxton No. 5.
Etruscan No. 5.
Roman Rimmed.

Class F, One Color.
Aetna Ornamented Nos. 1 and 3.
Arcadian Open.
Belgian Ornamented No. 2.
Celtic Ornamented.
Celtic No. 1.
Clarendon Ornamented.
Doric No. 1.
Florentine.
Ornate.
Ornate No. 2.
Renaissance No. 1.
Streamer Aetna.

Class G, One Color.
Caxton No. 4.
Etruscan No. 2.

Class B, Each Color.
Chromatic Streamer Gothic Cond. No. 4.

Class D, Each Color.
Chrom. Str. Antique Tuscan No. 3.
" " Antique Tuscan Condensed.
" " Arabian No. 1.
" " Etruscan No. 4.
" " Gothic Pointed.
" " Gothic Dotted.
" " Gothic Tuscan No. 3.
" " Gothic Tuscan Extra Cond.
" " Ionian.

Class E, Each Color.
Chrom. Aetna.
" Antique Tuscan Shade Nos. 1, 2.
" Corinthian No. 1.
" Etruscan No. 1.
" Gothic Tuscan.
" Old English Ornamented No. 3.
" Streamer Arcadian No. 1.

Class F, Each Color.
Chrom. Belgian Ornamented.
" Doric Ornamented.
" French Clarendon Ornamented.
" Gothic Paneled.
" Gothic Paneled No. 2.
" Old English Ornamented No. 8.

Class G, Each Color.
Chrom. Caxton.
" Corinthian.
" Etruscan No. 3.
" Ionian No. 2.
" Ionian No. 4.

Class B, E and F.
Chromatic Aetna No. 3.

Class B and E.
Chromatic Aldine Ornamented.

Class D and C.
Chromatic Celtic Ornamented.

Class E and C.
Chrom. French Clarendon Ornamented Nos. 4 and 5.
" Gothic Ornamented No. 7.

Class F and D.
Chromatic Arcadian Open.
" Arcadian Shaded.
" Renaissance.
" Streamer Gothic Paneled.

Class F and E.
Chromatic Aetna No. 1 and 2.
" French Clarendon Orna. No. 4.
" French Clarendon Orna. No. 6.
" Streamer Aetna No. 2.

Class F and A.
Chromatic Expanded Nos. 1 and 2.

Class F and B.
Chrom. Aetna No. 4.
" American.
" Clarendon Ornamented No. 6.
" Clarendon Ornamented.
" Doric.
" French Clarendon Orna. No. 2.
" Florentine.
" Gothic Paneled No. 1.
" Ornate.
" Ornate No. 2.
" Streamer Aetna No. 1.

Class G and E.
Chromatic Ionian No. 3.

Class G and B.
Chromatic Ionian No. 5.

Class H and B.
Chromatic Gothic Ornamented No. 1.
" Mexican.

Lines Pica	Class A Cents	Class B Cents	Class C Cents	Class D Cents	Class E Cents	Class F Cents	Class G Cents	Class H Cents
2	6	5	0	0	0	00	00	00
3	6	5	0	0	7	10	00	00
4	6	5	0	6	7	10	12	00
5	7	5	0	6	8	10	13	00
6	8	6	5	7	9	11	14	16
7	9	7	6	8	10	12	15	17
8	10	8	7	9	11	13	16	18
9	11	9	8	10	12	14	17	19
10	12	10	9	11	13	15	18	20
12	15	12	10	13	15	17	20	22
14	18	14	11	15	17	19	22	24
15	20	15	12	16	18	20	23	26
16	22	16	13	17	19	21	24	28
18	24	18	14	18	20	23	26	30
20	26	20	15	19	22	25	28	32
22	28	22	16	20	24	26	30	36
24	30	24	17	22	26	28	32	40
25	32	25	18	23	27	29	34	42
26	34	26	19	24	28	30	36	43
28	37	28	20	26	30	32	38	45
30	40	30	21	28	32	35	40	48
32	43	32	22	30	35	37	42	50
36 or 6 inches.	36	24	33	38	40	45	55	
40	40	26	35	42	45	50	60	
45	45	30	38	46	50	55	65	
50	50	35	42	52	55	60	70	
55	57	37	48	60	64	70	80	
60 or 10 inches.	65	40	55	70	72	80	90	
65	72	44	62	80	82	90	1 00	
72 or 12 inches.	80	50	70	90	92	1 00	1 10	
80	90	58	80	1 00	1 05	1 10	1 22	
90 or 15 inches.	1 00	67	90	1 12	1 18	1 22	1 35	
100		75	1 00					
110		84	1 12					
120 or 20 inches.		95	1 25					

For all sizes larger than 120 lines Pica, special prices on application.

When less than 25 letters are ordered of any one style, the price will be 50 per cent extra.

This Price List and Scale of Fonts, is arranged especially for articles shown in this book. It will be seen that we have arranged a 2 A font, for those only wanting a small quantity, and make no lower case or figures in two colors.

Scale of Fonts

	2 A Capitals. 52 LETTERS.	3 A Capitals. 75 LETTERS.	4 A Capitals. 106 LETTERS.	5 A Capitals. 129 LETTERS.
A	2	3	3	3
B	2	2	3	3
C	2	3	3	4
D	2	2	3	4
E	3	4	5	6
F	2	2	3	3
G	2	2	3	3
H	2	2	3	4
I	2	4	4	4
J	2	2	2	3
K	1	1	2	2
L	2	2	3	4
M	1	2	3	3
N	2	3	4	5
O	2	3	4	5
P	2	2	2	3
Q	1	2	2	2
R	2	3	4	5
S	2	3	4	5
T	2	2	2	4
U	2	2	3	3
V	1	2	2	3
W	1	1	2	3
X	1	1	2	2
Y	1	1	2	2
Z	1	1	2	2
&	1	1	2	2
!	2	2	2	3
.	2	2	3	4
-	2	1	1	1
,	1	2	2	3
:		1	2	2
;		1	1	2
;		3	3	4

PRICES OF BORDERS PER FOOT.
No. 17, $2 02 Complete in Colors.
" 18, 1 75 One Color.
" 25, 3 00 Complete in Colors.
" 28, 3 00 "
" 29, 3 00 "
" 34, 70 "
" 36, 1 50 "
" 38, 1 00 One Color.
" 39, 3 50 Complete in Colors.
" 40, 3 00 "
" 41, 1 50 One Color.
" 42, 2 03 Complete in Colors.
" 43, 2 50 "
" 44, 2 50 "
" 45, 1 87 "
" 46, 1 87 "
" 47, 1 25 One Color.
" 48, 3 50 Complete in Colors.
" 51, 3 00 "
" 52, 1 25 One Color.
" 53, 2 75 Complete in Colors.
" 54, 1 00 One Color.
" 55, 75 Complete in Colors.

No. 56, 1 00 One Color.
" 57, 1 00 "
" 58, 2 00 Complete in Colors.
" 59, 2 00 "
" 60, 75 One Color.
" 61, 1 50 Complete in Colors.
" 62, 1 00 One Color.
" 63, 2 25 Complete in Colors.
" 66, 1 50 One Color.
" 67, 3 00 Per set of Corners, Rule, 30 Cents per Foot, Complete in Colors.
" 68, 3 00 Complete in Colors.
" 69, 2 75 "
" 70, 2 00 "
" 71, 2 00 "
" 72, 2 00 "
" 73, 1 25 One Color.
" 74, 2 00 Complete in Colors.
" 75, 2 00 "
" 76, 1 75 "
" 77, 1 50 "
" 78, 1 00 One Color.
" 79, 2 00 One Color.

Grecian Border. One Color, $1 50
" No. 1. " 1 00
" " 5. " 1 25
" " 6. " 1 25
Chain " Complete for Colors. 3 00
" " No. 1. One Color. 1 50
" " 2. " 1 50
" " 3. " 1 00
" " 4. Complete. 2 00
" " 5. " 2 00
" " 6. " 2 00
" " 7. " 2 00
" " 8. " 2 00
National " " 3 00
Circus " " 3 00
" " Nos. 1 & 2. One Color. 1 50
Mosaic " " 1 75
" " 1. Complete. 2 50
Ring " One Color. 1 50
" " One Color. 1 00
Rustic "
Scroll Border. Corners and Center pieces $6 00 per set of four each. Rule on same body as Center pieces, 40 cents per foot, complete for two colors.

TERMS OF SALE. On all purchases for less amount than $100, net cash, payable on receipt of goods; on purchases exceeding $100, four months for approved bankable paper, or 5 per cent. off for cash.

Boxwood, Maple, Mahogany and Pine, prepared for Wood Engravers. Mahogany and Cherry Blocking for Stereotypers. Also, all kinds of bleachers's Type and Stamps made to order.

We can furnish any style or size of Wood Type made, and if you do not see what pleases you in this Book, order from any other, and mention what Book.

All Type of our make, are marked on the A's of each font, "WM. H. PAGE & CO.," and all bearing this stamp, are warranted to give entire satisfaction in all cases.

We would particularly request our patrons not to cut or mutilate this book, as the names and numbers written out in full, and in a plain hand, will be a sufficient guarantee of their obtaining what they want.

Ten Line Chain Border No. 7. $2,00 per foot Complete.

MANUFACTURED BY

Wm. H. Page & Co.

STARS, Cut any size desired.

12 Line Star No. 2. Class G. 20 Cents.   12 Line Star No. 4. Class H. 22 Cents.   12 Line Star No. 3. Double Class H. 44 Cents.

12 Line Star No. 5. Class H. 22 Cents.   Star Rule Corners, 25 Cents per Set.   12 Line Star No. 1. Class B. 12 Cents.

STAR RULE, 20 Cents per Foot.

No. 9.   No. 10.

No. 2.   No. 3.

No. 5.   No. 6.

No. 1.   No. 4.

No. 7.   No. 8.

No. 11.   No. 12.

Six Line Border No. 69. $2,75 per foot, complete.

Six Line Border No. 77. $1,50 per foot, complete.

Wm. H. Page & Co.

FANCY RULE, cut in short pieces on end wood, with mitered corners.   Price, from No's. 21 to 50, 50 Cents per foot.

No. 4   10 Cents per Foot.

No. 5   15 Cents.

No. 6   20 Cents.

No. 7   22 Cents.

No. 8   25 Cents.

No. 9   30 Cents.

No. 10   35 Cents.

No. 11   45 Cents.

No. 12   10 Cents.

No. 13   15 Cents.

No. 14   20 Cents.

No. 15   22 Cents.

No. 16   25 Cents.

No. 17   30 Cents.

No. 18   35 Cents.

No. 19   40 Cents.

No. 20   45 Cents.

No. 21.

No. 22.

No. 23.

No. 24.

No. 25.

No. 26.

No. 27.

No. 28.

No. 29.

No. 30.

No. 31.

No. 32.

No. 33.

No. 34.

No. 35.

No. 36.

No. 37.

No. 38.

No. 39.

No. 40.

No. 41.

No. 42.

No. 43.

No. 44.

No. 45.

No. 46.

No. 47.

No. 48.

No. 49.

No. 50.

In ordering, leave out no part of the name or number printed over the line.

[Patented.]   Nine Line Aetna Open.   Class E.   12 Cents.

CROQUET

Twelve Line Aetna Open.   Class E.   15 Cents.

STORM

Eighteen Line Aetna Open.   Class E.   20 Cents.

HUB

Twenty-four Line Aetna Open.   Class E.   26 Cents.

NIT

Printed with WADE'S INKS, from H. D. Wade & Co., 50 Ann St., New York.

In ordering, leave out no part of the name or number printed over the line.

[Patented.]   Fifteen Line Caxton No. 5.   Class E.   18 Cents.

KINGDOM

Twenty Line Caxton No. 5.   Class E.   22 Cents.

MOUND

Thirty Line Caxton No. 5.   Class E.   32 Cents.

SIZE

Printed with WADE'S INKS, from H. D. Wade & Co., 50 Ann St., New York.

Manufactured by Wm. H. Page & Co.

In ordering, leave out no part of the name or number printed over the line.

| Nine Line Caxton No. 4. | Class G.   17 Cents. |

[Patented.]

GEOGRAPHICAL

| Twelve Line Caxton No. 4. | Class G.   20 Cents. |

EXCURSION

| Eighteen Line Caxton No. 4. | Class G.   26 Cents. |

KNIVES

| Twenty-four Line Caxton No. 4. | Class G.   32 Cents. |

HOME

Printed with WADE'S INKS, from H. D. Wade & Co., 50 Ann St., New York.

In ordering, leave out no part of the name or number printed over the line.

Sixteen Line Arcadian No. 1 Open.   Class E.   19 Cents.

ENORMOUS

Twenty Line Arcadian Open.   Class F.   25 Cents.

SORTING

Thirty Line Arcadian No. 1 Open.   Class E.   32 Cents.

THEM

Printed with WADE'S INKS, from H. D. Wade & Co., 50 Ann St., New York.

Manufactured by Wm. H. Page & Co.

In ordering, leave out no part of the name or number printed over the line.

Nine Line Celtic No. 1.   Class F. 14 Cents.

[Patented.]

DEMORALIZED ORGANIZATION

Twelve Line Celtic No. 1.   Class F. 17 Cents.

PUBLIC INDORSEMENT

Eighteen Line Celtic No. 1.   Class F. 23 Cents.

IMPROVEMENT

Twenty-four Line Celtic No. 1.   Class F. 28 Cents.

STEAMERS!

Printed with WADE'S INKS, from H. D. Wade & Co., 50 Ann St., New York.

In ordering, leave out no part of the name or number printed over the line.

[Patented.]   Nine Line Etruscan No. 2.   Class G.   17 Cents.

HANDSOME PICTURE

Twelve Line Etruscan No. 2.   Class G.   20 Cents.

DARK FORESTS

Eighteen Line Etruscan No. 2.   Class G.   26 Cents.

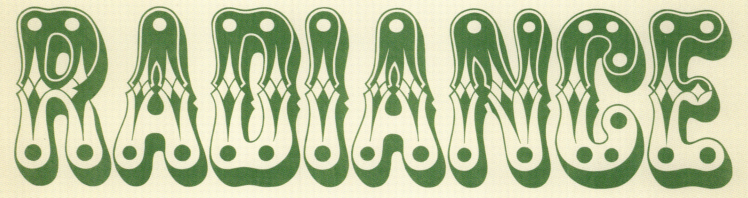

RADIANCE

Twenty-four Line Etruscan No. 2.   Class G.   32 Cents.

MOSAIC

Printed with WADE'S INKS, from H. D. Wade & Co., 50 Ann St., New York.

In ordering, leave out no part of the name or number printed over the line.

Nine Line Aetna Ornamented.   Class E.   12 Cents.

[Patented.]

KITCHEN

Twelve Line Aetna Ornamented No. 1.   Class F.   17 Cents.

ROUND

Eighteen Line Aetna Ornamented No. 2.   Class E.   20 Cents.

BITS

Twenty-four Line Aetna Ornamented No. 3.   Class F.   28 Cents.

SIN

Printed with WADE'S INKS, from H. D. Wade & Co., 50 Ann St., New York.

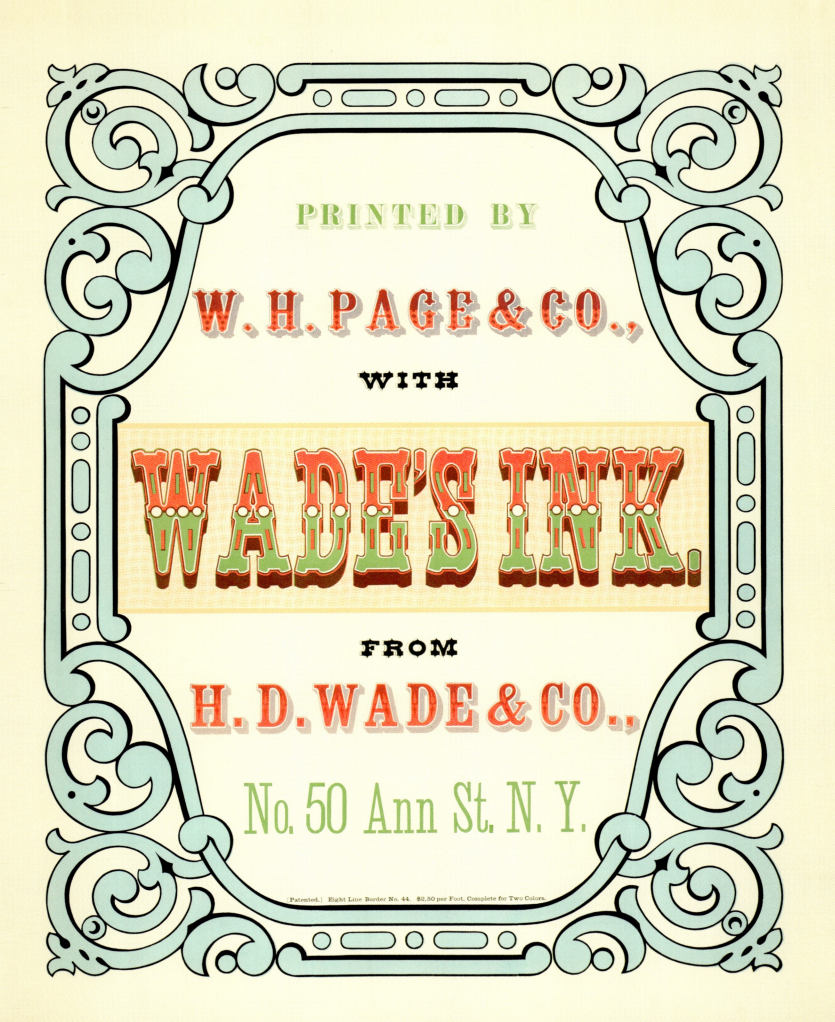

PRINTED BY

W. H. PAGE & CO.,

WITH

WADE'S INK.

FROM

H. D. WADE & CO.,

No. 50 Ann St. N. Y.

[Patented.] Eight Line Border No. 44. $2,50 per Foot, Complete for Two Colors.

In ordering, leave out no part of the name or number printed over the line.

Nine Line Chromatic Caxton.　　　　　　　　Class G.　17 Cents, Each Color.

[Patented.]

GEOGRAPHICAL

Twelve Line Chromatic Caxton.　　　　　　　　Class G.　20 Cents, Each Color.

EXCURSION

Eighteen Line Chromatic Caxton.　　　　　　　　Class G.　26 Cents, Each Color.

KNIVES

Twenty-four Line Chromatic Caxton.　　　　　　　　Class G.　32 Cents, Each Color.

HOME

Printed with WADE'S INKS, from H. D. Wade & Co., 50 Ann St., New York.

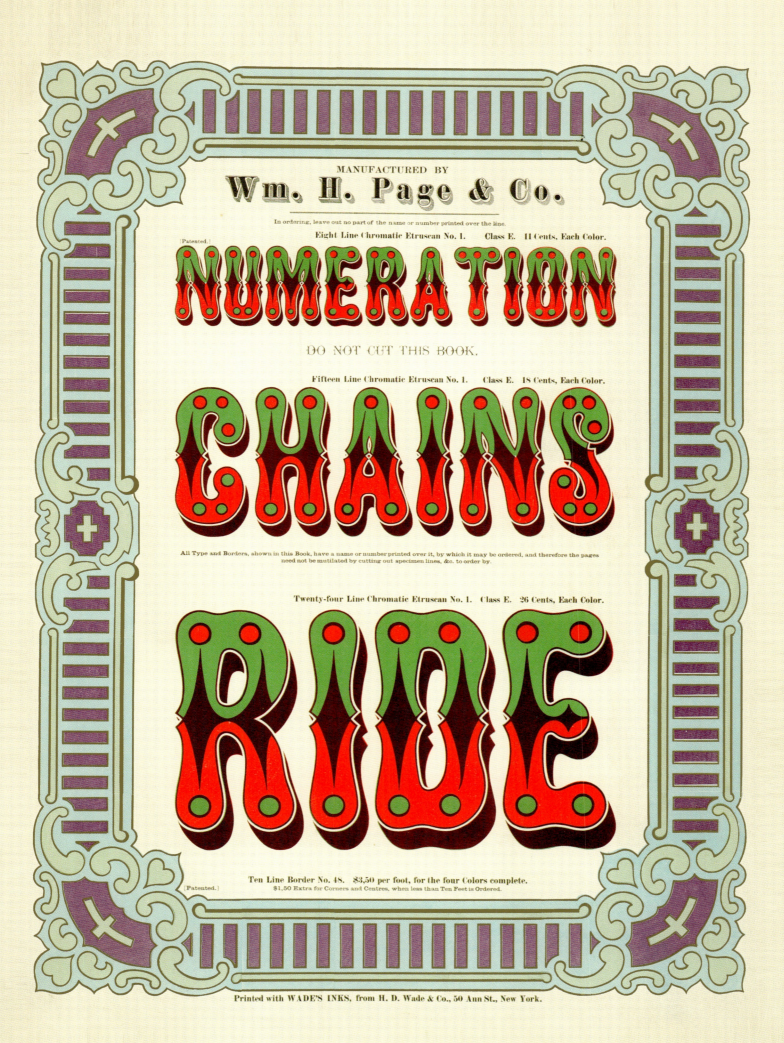

MANUFACTURED BY

Wm. H. Page & Co.

In ordering, leave out no part of the name or number printed over the line.

Eight Line Chromatic Etruscan No. 1.   Class E.   11 Cents, Each Color.

[Patented.]

NUMERATION

DO NOT CUT THIS BOOK.

Fifteen Line Chromatic Etruscan No. 1.   Class E.   18 Cents, Each Color.

CHAINS

All Type and Borders, shown in this Book, have a name or number printed over it, by which it may be ordered, and therefore the pages need not be mutilated by cutting out specimen lines, &c. to order by.

Twenty-four Line Chromatic Etruscan No. 1.   Class E.   26 Cents, Each Color.

RIDE

Ten Line Border No. 48. $3,50 per foot, for the four Colors complete.

[Patented.] $1,50 Extra for Corners and Centres, when less than Ten Feet is Ordered.

Printed with WADE'S INKS, from H. D. Wade & Co., 50 Ann St., New York.

In ordering, leave out no part of the name or number printed over the line.

[Patented.]

Sixteen Line Chromatic Arcadian Open.

Outside, Class F. 21 Cents.
Inset, Class D. 17 Cents.

Twenty Line Chromatic Arcadian Open.

Outside, Class F. 25 Cents.
Inset, Class D. 19 Cents.

Thirty Line Chromatic Arcadian Open.

Outside, Class F. 35 Cents.
Inset, Class D. 28 Cents.

ERUDITION

BLUSTER

PINES

Printed with WADE'S INKS, from H. D. Wade & Co., 50 Ann St., New York.

Manufactured by Wm. H. Page & Co.

In ordering, leave out no part of the name or number printed over the line.

[Patented.]

Nine Line Chromatic Etruscan No. 3.   Class G.   17 Cents, Each Color.

Twelve Line Chromatic Etruscan No. 3.   Class G.   20 Cents, Each Color.

Eighteen Line Chromatic Etruscan No. 3.   Class G.   26 Cents, Each Color.

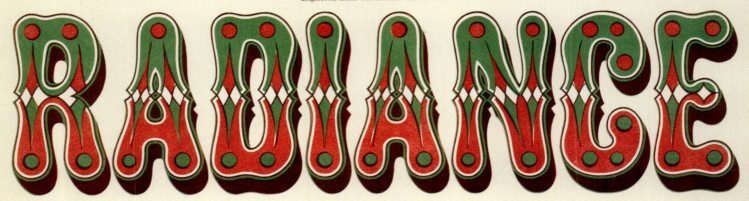

Twenty-four Line Chromatic Etruscan No. 3.   Class G.   32 Cents, Each Color.

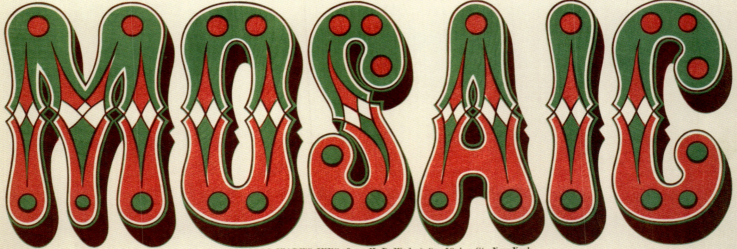

Printed with WADE'S INKS, from H. D. Wade & Co., 50 Ann St., New York.

In ordering, leave out no part of the name or No. printed over the line.

Nine Line Chromatic Aetna No. 1.

Outside, Class F. 14 Cents.
Inset, Class E. 12 Cents.

LIGHTER

Twelve Line Chromatic Aetna No. 1.

Outside, Class F. 17 Cents.
Inset, Class E. 15 Cents.

HOURS

Eighteen Line Chromatic Aetna No. 1.

Outside, Class F. 23 Cents.
Inset, Class E. 20 Cents.

BITS

Twenty-four Line Chromatic Aetna No. 1.

Outside, Class F. 28 Cents.
Inset, Class E. 26 Cents.

SIN

Printed with WADE'S INKS, from H. D. Wade & Co., 50 Ann St., New York.

In ordering, leave out no part of the name or No. printed over the line.

Nine Line Chromatic Aetna No. 2.	Outside, Class F. 14 Cents. Inset, Class E. 12 Cents.

KITCHEN

Twelve Line Chromatic Aetna No. 2.	Outside, Class F. 17 Cents. Inset, Class E. 15 Cents.

ROUND

Eighteen Line Chromatic Aetna No. 2.	Outside, Class F. 23 Cents. Inset, Class E. 20 Cents.

ZINC

Twenty-four Line Chromatic Aetna No. 2.	Outside, Class F. 28 Cents. Inset, Class E. 26 Cents.

TIE

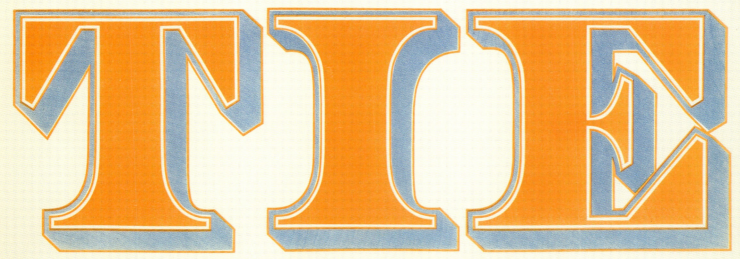

Printed with WADE'S INKS, from H. D. Wade & Co., 50 Ann St., New York.

35

In ordering, leave out no part of the name or No. printed over the line.

Nine Line Chromatic Aetna.

Class E. 12 Cents, Each Color.

[Patented.]

LIGHTER

Twelve Line Chromatic Aetna.

Class E. 15 Cents, Each Color.

HOURS

Eighteen Line Chromatic Aetna.

Class E. 20 Cents, Each Color.

BITS

Twenty-four Line Chromatic Aetna.

Class E. 26 Cents, Each Color.

SIN

Printed with WADE'S INKS, from H. D. Wade & Co., 50 Ann St., New York.

In ordering, leave out no part of the name or number printed over the line.

[Patented.]

Nine Line Chromatic Aetna No. 3.

Yellow, Class B.	9 Cents.
Gold, Class E.	12 Cents.
Black, Class F.	14 Cents.

Twelve Line Chromatic Aetna No. 3.

Yellow, Class B.	12 Cents.
Gold, Class E.	15 Cents.
Black, Class F.	17 Cents.

Eighteen Line Chromatic Aetna No. 3.

Yellow, Class B.	18 Cents.
Gold, Class E.	20 Cents.
Black, Class F.	23 Cents.

Twenty-four Line Chromatic Aetna No. 3.

Yellow, Class B.	24 Cents.
Gold, Class E.	26 Cents.
Black, Class F.	28 Cents.

LIGHTER
HOURS
BITS
SIN

Printed with WADE'S INKS, from H. D. Wade & Co., 50 Ann St., New York.

Manufactured by Wm. H. Page & Co.

In ordering, leave out no part of the name or number printed over the line.

Ten Line Chromatic Aetna No. 3.

[Patented.]

Black, Class F. 15 Cents.
Green, Class E. 13 Cents.
Gold, Class B. 10 Cents.

BLEACH

Fourteen Line Chromatic Aetna No. 3.

50 Cents per Letter, complete.

TIDES

Sixteen Line Chromatic Aetna No. 3.

56 Cents per Letter, complete.

MOST

Twenty Line Chromatic Aetna No. 3.

67 Cents per Letter, complete.

RED

Printed with WADE'S INKS, from H. D. Wade & Co., 50 Ann St., New York.

TINT No. 13.

MANUFACTURED BY

Wm. H. Page & Co.

GREENEVILLE, CONN.

Two Line Border No. 61. $1,50 per foot, complete.

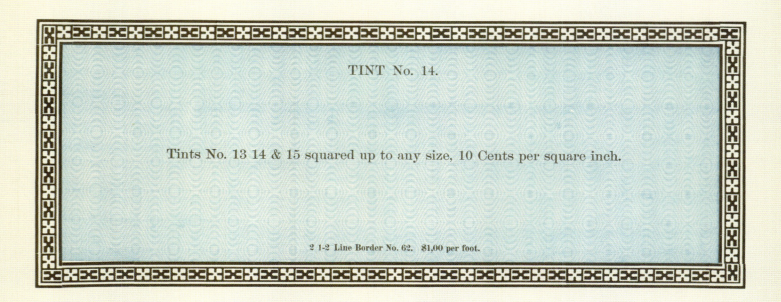

TINT No. 14.

Tints No. 13 14 & 15 squared up to any size, 10 Cents per square inch.

2 1-2 Line Border No. 62. $1,00 per foot.

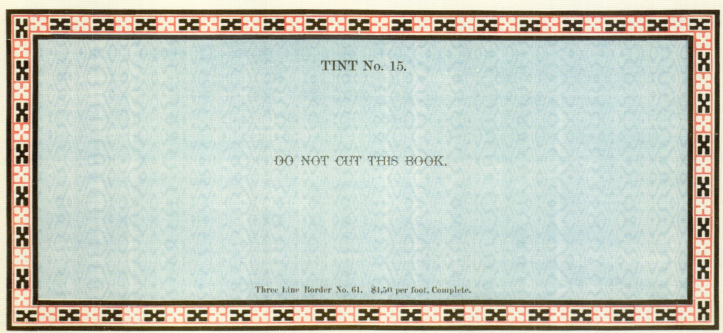

TINT No. 15.

DO NOT CUT THIS BOOK.

Three Line Border No. 61. $1,50 per foot, Complete.

Printed with WADE'S INKS, from H. D. Wade & Co., 50 Ann St., New York.

TINT No. 7.

MANUFACTURED BY

Wm. H. Page & Co.

GREENEVILLE, CONN.

Three Line Border No. 65. $1,50 per foot.

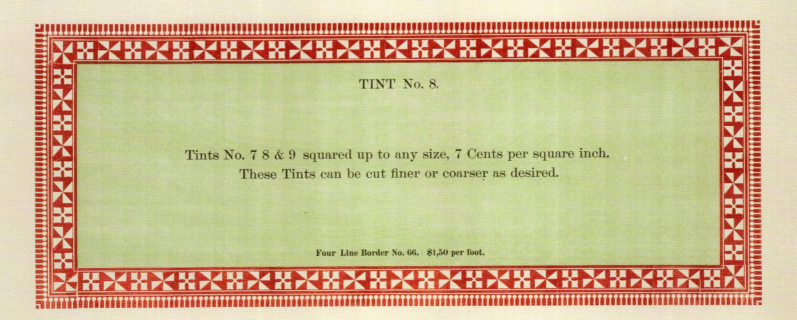

TINT No. 8.

Tints No. 7 8 & 9 squared up to any size, 7 Cents per square inch.
These Tints can be cut finer or coarser as desired.

Four Line Border No. 66. $1,50 per foot.

TINT No. 9.

Five Line Border No. 66. $1,50 per foot.

Printed with WADE'S INKS, from H. D. Wade & Co., 50 Ann St., New York.

TINT No. 10.

MANUFACTURED BY

Wm. H. Page & Co.

GREENEVILLE, CONN.

Four Line Border No. 61. $1.50 per foot, complete.

TINT No. 11.

Tints No. 10 11 & 12 squared up to any size, 10 Cents per square inch.

Five Line Border No. 62. $1.00 per foot.

TINT No. 12.

Six Line Border No. 61. $1.50 per foot, Complete.

Printed with WADE'S INKS, from H. D. Wade & Co., 50 Ann St., New York.

TINT No. 4.

MANUFACTURED BY

Wm. H. Page & Co.

GREENEVILLE, CONN.

Seven Line Border No. 43. $2.50 per foot for two Colors complete.
$1.00 extra for Corners and Centers, when less than Ten Feet are ordered.

(Patented.)

TINT No. 5.

Tint No. 4 squared up to any size, 7 Cents per square inch.
" " 5 " " " " " 10 " " " "
" " 6 " " " " " 10 " " " "
These Tints can be cut finer or coarser as desired.

TINT No. 6.

Eight Line Border No. 29. $3.00 per foot for the three Colors complete.
$1.50 extra for Corners and Centers, when less than Ten Feet is Ordered.

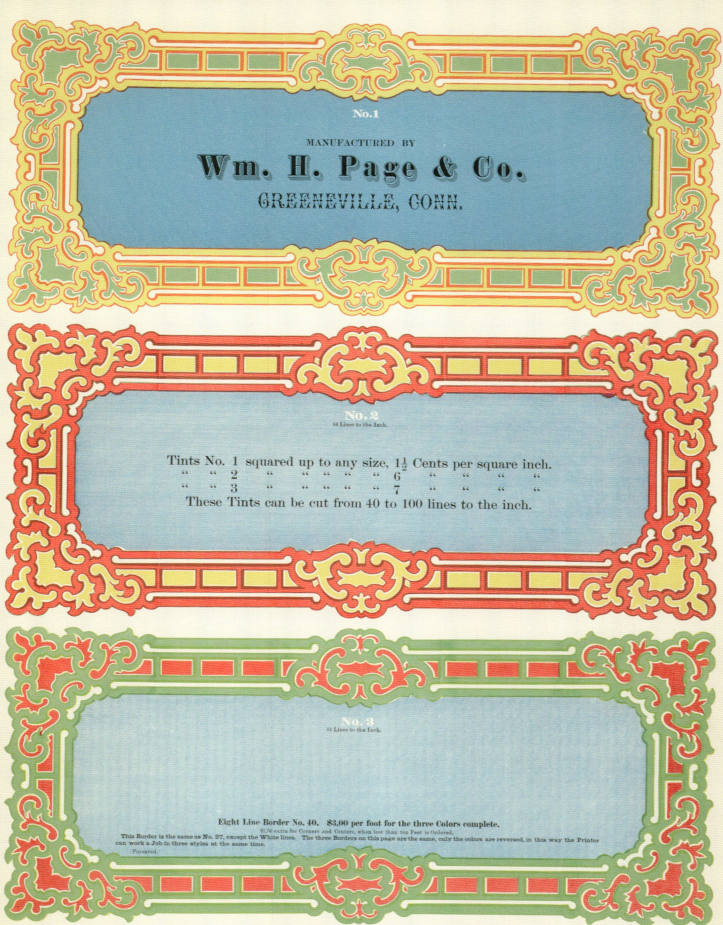

No. 1

MANUFACTURED BY

Wm. H. Page & Co.
GREENEVILLE, CONN.

No. 2

64 Lines to the Inch.

Tints No. 1 squared up to any size, 1½ Cents per square inch.
" " 2 " " " " " 6 " " " "
" " 3 " " " " " 7 " " " "
These Tints can be cut from 40 to 100 lines to the inch.

No. 3

64 Lines to the Inch.

Eight Line Border No. 40. $3.00 per foot for the three Colors complete.

$1.50 extra for Corners and Centers, when less than ten Feet is Ordered.

This Border is the same as No. 27, except the White lines. The three Borders on this page are the same, only the colors are reversed, in this way the Printer can work a Job in three styles at the same time.

Patented.

Printed with WADE'S INKS, from H. D. Wade & Co., 50 Ann St., New York.

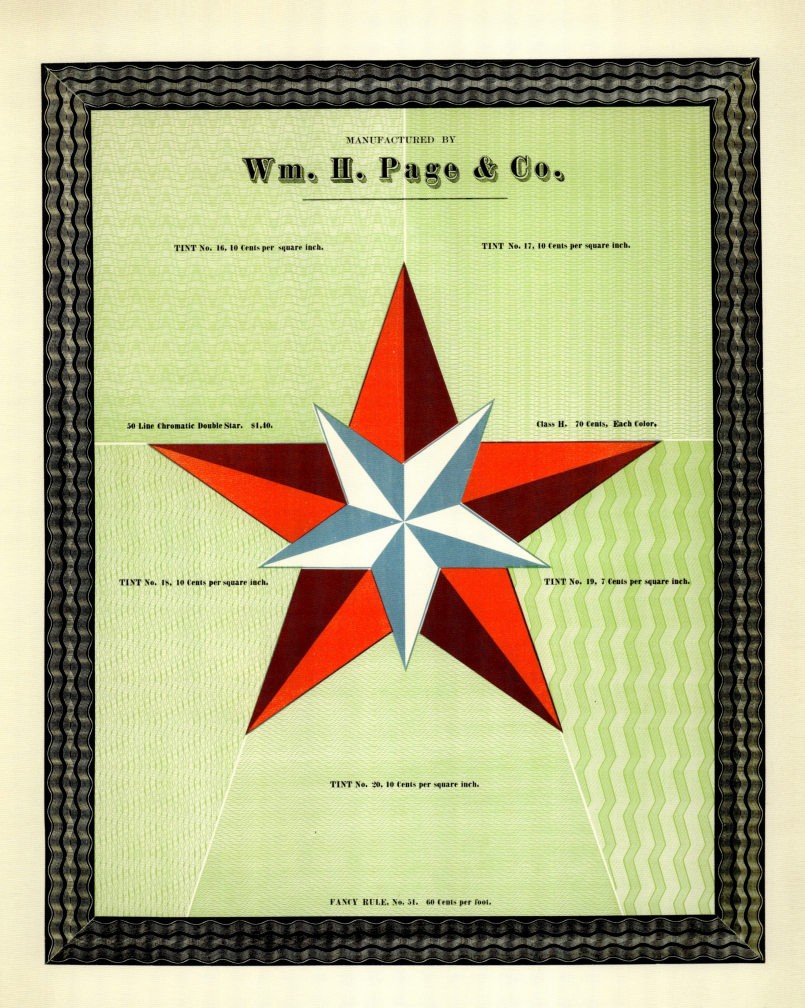

MANUFACTURED BY

Wm. H. Page & Co.

TINT No. 16, 10 Cents per square inch.

TINT No. 17, 10 Cents per square inch.

50 Line Chromatic Double Star. $1,40.

Class H. 70 Cents, Each Color.

TINT No. 18, 10 Cents per square inch.

TINT No. 19, 7 Cents per square inch.

TINT No. 20, 10 Cents per square inch.

FANCY RULE, No. 51. 60 Cents per foot.

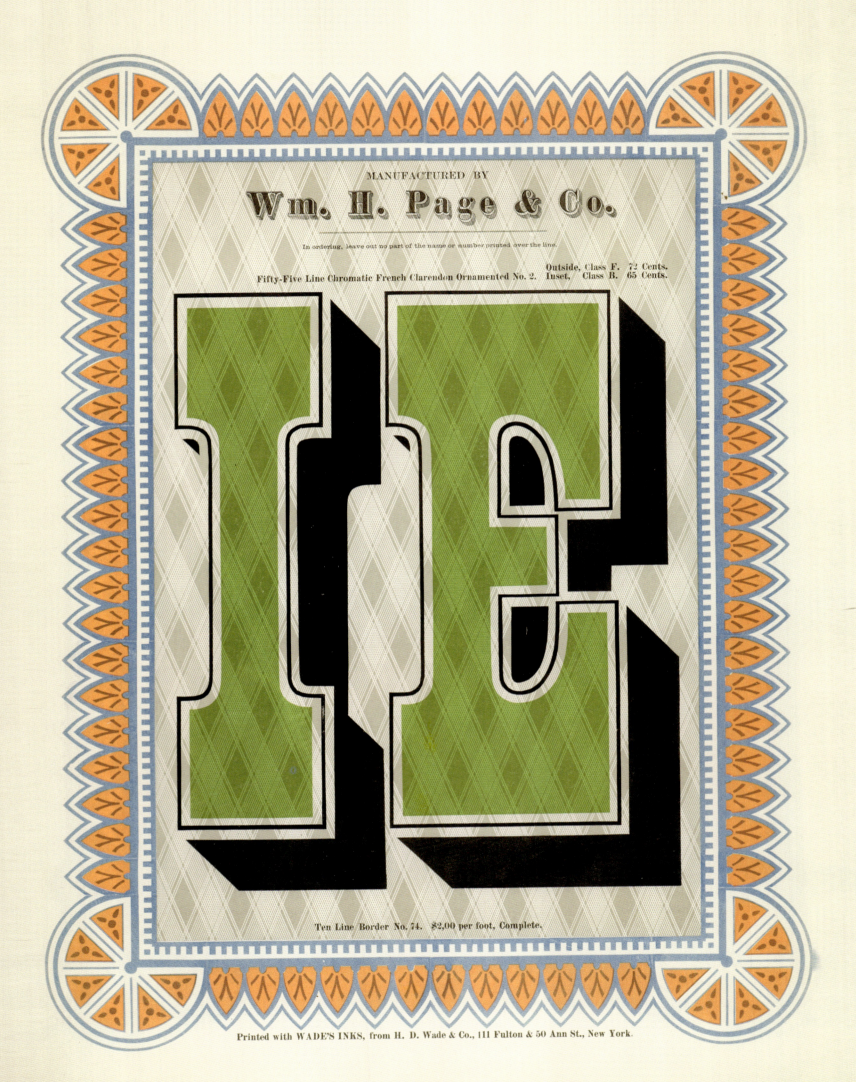

MANUFACTURED BY

Wm. H. Page & Co.

In ordering, leave out no part of the name or number printed over the line.

Fifty-Five Line Chromatic French Clarendon Ornamented No. 2. Outside, Class F. 72 Cents. Inset, Class B. 65 Cents.

Ten Line Border No. 74. $2,00 per foot, Complete.

Printed with WADE'S INKS, from H. D. Wade & Co., 111 Fulton & 50 Ann St., New York.

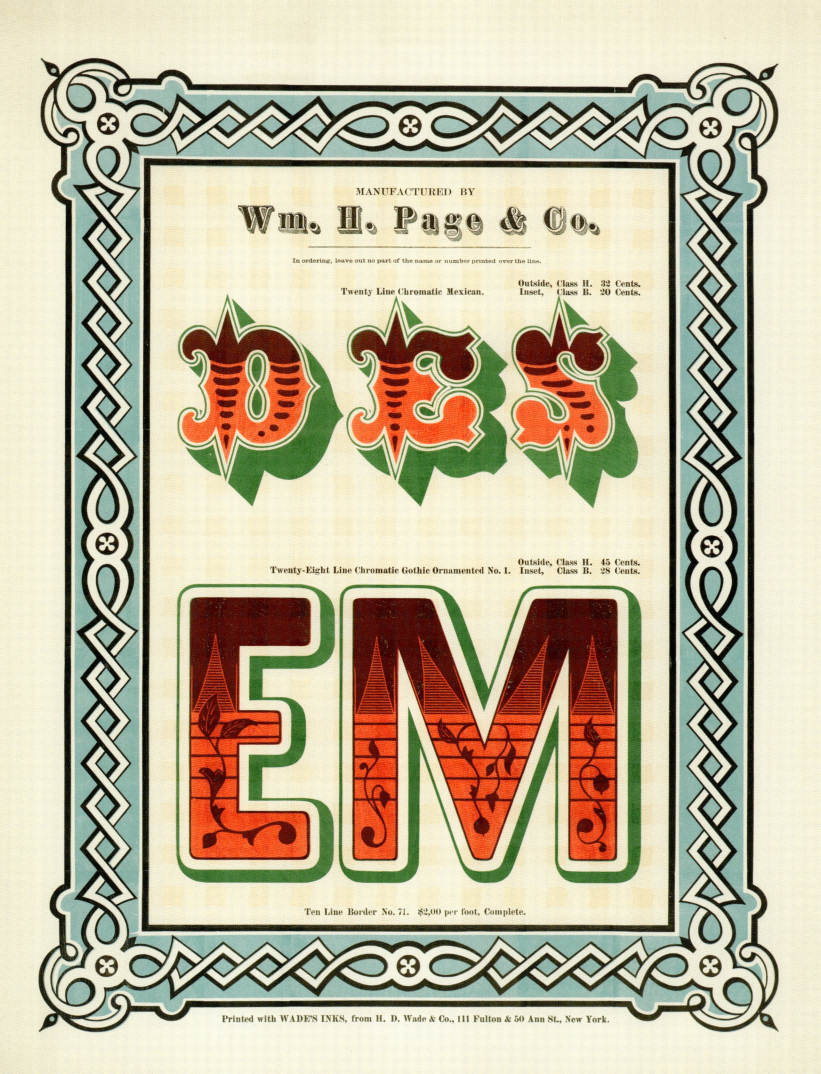

MANUFACTURED BY

Wm. H. Page & Co.

In ordering, leave out no part of the name or number printed over the line.

Twenty Line Chromatic Mexican.　　Outside, Class H. 32 Cents.
　　　　　　　　　　　　　　　　Inset,　Class B. 20 Cents.

Twenty-Eight Line Chromatic Gothic Ornamented No. 1.　Outside, Class H. 45 Cents.
　　　　　　　　　　　　　　　　　　　　　　　Inset,　Class B. 28 Cents.

Ten Line Border No. 71.　$2,00 per foot, Complete.

Printed with WADE'S INKS, from H. D. Wade & Co., 111 Fulton & 50 Ann St., New York.

MANUFACTURED BY

Wm. H. Page & Co.

In ordering, leave out no part of the name or number printed over the line.

Twelve Line Chromatic Gothic Tuscan. Class E. 15 Cents, Each Color.

HEM

Twelve Line Chromatic Antique Tuscan Shade No's 1 & 2. Class E. 15 Cents, Each Color.

RUG

Twenty Line Chromatic Antique Tuscan Shade No's 1 & 2. Class E. 22 Cents, Each Color.

SG

Twelve Line Border No. 42. $2,00 per foot, Complete.

Printed with WADE'S INKS, from H. D. Wade & Co., 111 Fulton & 50 Ann St., New York.

MANUFACTURED BY

Wm. H. Page & Co.

GREENEVILLE, CONN.

Six Line Block Tints No. 1.   Class C.   5 Cents Each.
These Tints cut any size desired.   Blanks free.

[Patented.]

Four Line Border No. 57. $1,00 per foot.

Six Line Border No. 63. $2,25 per foot, Complete.

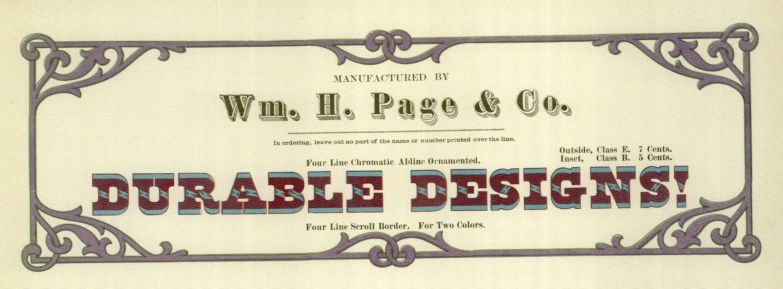

MANUFACTURED BY

Wm. H. Page & Co.

In ordering, leave out no part of the name or number printed over the line.

Four Line Chromatic Aldine Ornamented.

Outside, Class E. 7 Cents.
Inset, Class B. 5 Cents.

DURABLE DESIGNS!

Four Line Scroll Border. For Two Colors.

Corners and Center pieces, $6,00 per set of four each, complete. Rule cut on same body as the Center pieces, 40 cents per foot, complete. All sizes the same price.

Six Line Chromatic Aldine Ornamented.

Outside, Class E. 9 Cents.
Inset, Class B. 6 Cents.

WORSHIPERS

Five Line Scroll Border. For Two Colors.

In ordering an addition to any Border, it will always be necessary to send one piece of each color of the blocks to match by.

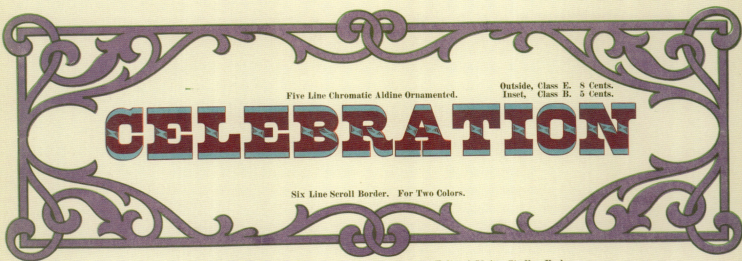

Five Line Chromatic Aldine Ornamented.

Outside, Class E. 8 Cents.
Inset, Class B. 5 Cents.

CELEBRATION

Six Line Scroll Border. For Two Colors.

Printed with WADE'S INKS, from H. D. Wade & Co., 111 Fulton & 50 Ann St., New York.

50

MANUFACTURED BY

Wm. H. Page & Co.

In ordering, leave out no part of the name or number printed over the line.

Three Line Chromatic Expanded No. 1.   Outside, Class F. 10 Cents.
Inset,   Class A.   6 Cents.

MERCHANTS

Six Line Ring Border. $1,50 per foot.

(Patented.)   Ten Line Chromatic Ionian No. 3.   Outside, Class G. 18 Cents.
Inset,   Class E. 13 Cents.

HIGHEST PRICE

Seven Line Ring Border. $1,50 per foot.

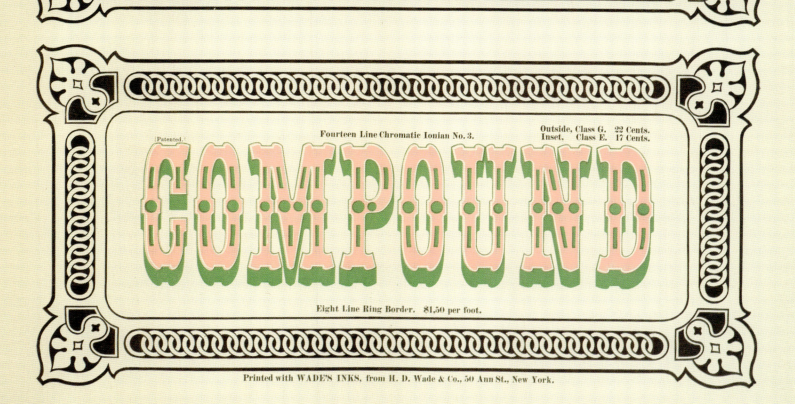

[Patented.]   Fourteen Line Chromatic Ionian No. 3.   Outside, Class G. 22 Cents.
Inset,   Class E. 17 Cents.

COMPOUND

Eight Line Ring Border. $1,50 per foot.

Printed with WADE'S INKS, from H. D. Wade & Co., 50 Ann St., New York.

MANUFACTURED BY

Wm. H. Page & Co.

In ordering, leave out no part of the name or number printed over the line.

Six Line Chromatic Antique Tuscan Shade Nos. 1 nnd 2.   Class E.   9 Cents, Each Color.

MINGLE

Six Line Chromatic Expanded No. 2.

Outside, Class F.   11 Censt.
Inset,   Class A.   8 Cents.

KIND

[Patented.]

Five Line Border No. 44. $2,50 per foot, complete for two Colors.

DO NOT CUT THIS BOOK.

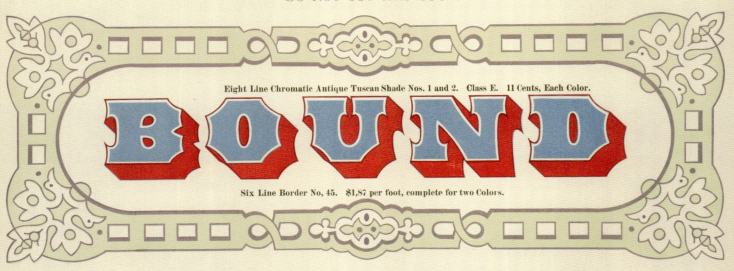

Eight Line Chromatic Antique Tuscan Shade Nos. 1 and 2.   Class E.   11 Cents, Each Color.

BOUND

Six Line Border No. 45. $1,87 per foot, complete for two Colors.

All Type and Borders, shown in this Book, have a name or number printed over it, by which it may be ordered, and therefore the pages need not be mutilated by cutting out specimen lines, &c. to order by.

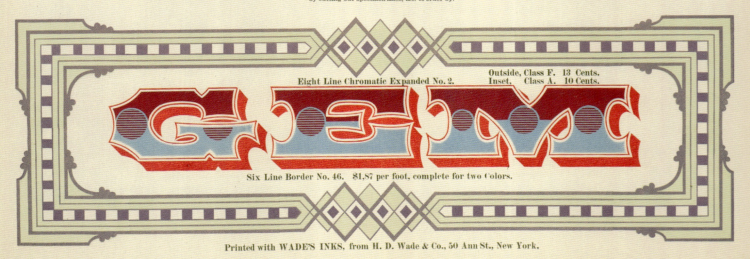

Eight Line Chromatic Expanded No. 2.

Outside, Class F.   13 Cents.
Inset,   Class A.   10 Cents.

GEM

Six Line Border No. 46. $1,87 per foot, complete for two Colors.

Printed with WADE'S INKS, from H. D. Wade & Co., 50 Ann St., New York.

MANUFACTURED BY

Wm. H. Page & Co.

Fifteen Line Florentine. Class F. 20 Cents.

GERM

(Patented Aug. 9, 1870.) Nine Line Chain Border No. 4. $2,00 per foot, complete for two colors.

These Chain Borders are cut from 4 to 20 lines Pica, in one two or three colors, as shown on this and other pages. Be particular in ordering to write all the names and Numbers in full. Each Color is a perfet Border when worked single.

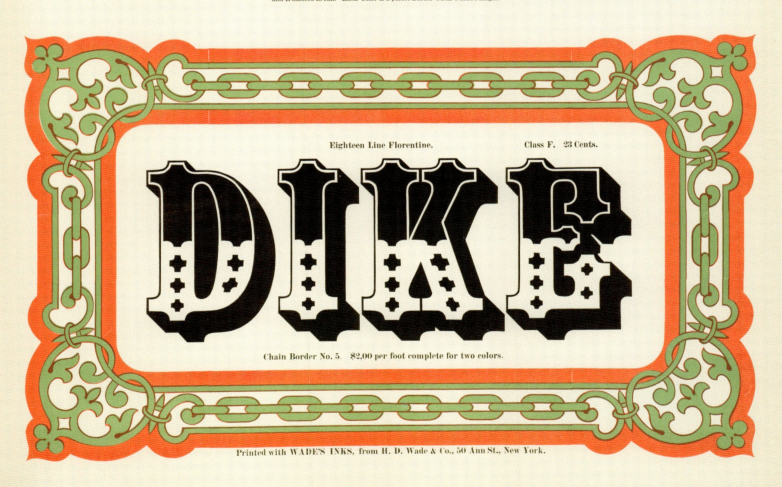

Eighteen Line Florentine. Class F. 23 Cents.

DIKE

Chain Border No. 5. $2,00 per foot complete for two colors.

Printed with WADE'S INKS, from H. D. Wade & Co., 50 Ann St., New York.

53

MANUFACTURED BY

Wm. H. Page & Co.

In ordering, leave out no part of the name or number printed over the line.

Fifteen Line Chromatic Florentine.　　　Outside, Class F.　20 Cents.
　　　　　　　　　　　　　　　　　　　　　Inset,　Class B.　15 Cents.

GERM

(Patented.)　Eight Line Border No. 28.　$3.00 per foot, complete for three Colors.

These Borders Cut from Eight to Twenty Lines Pica.　$2.00 Extra for Corners and Centres, when less than Ten Feet is Ordered.

Eighteen Line Chromatic Florentine.　　　Outside, Class F.　23 Cents.
　　　　　　　　　　　　　　　　　　　　　Inset,　Class B.　18 Cents.

DIKE

[Patented.]　Ten Line Border No. 25.　$3.00 per foot, complete for three Colors.

Printed with WADE'S INKS, from H. D. Wade & Co., 50 Ann St., New York.

54

MANUFACTURED BY

Wm. H. Page & Co.

(Patented.) Twenty-four Line Ornate. Class F. 28 Cents.

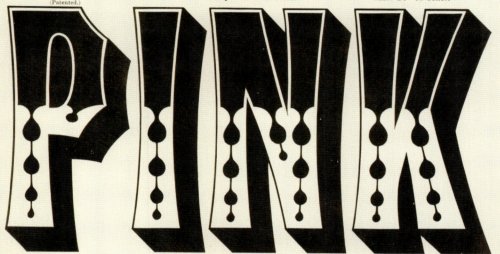

Thirty-two Line Ornate. Class F. 37 Cents.

Ten Line Ring Border No. 1. $2,25 per foot complete. Cut from 4 to 12 Lines Pica.

Printed with WADE'S INKS, from H. D. Wade & Co., 50 Ann St., New York.

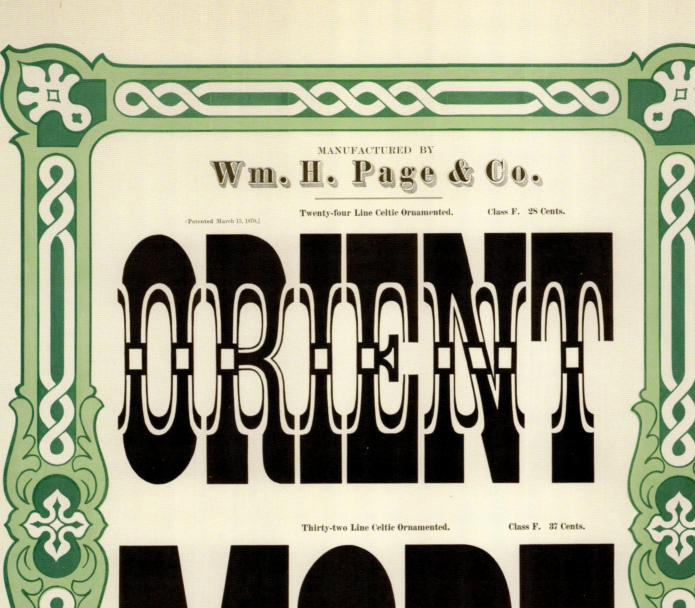

MANUFACTURED BY

Wm. H. Page & Co.

(Patented March 15, 1870.)　　Twenty-four Line Celtic Ornamented.　　Class F.　28 Cents.

ORIENT

Thirty-two Line Celtic Ornamented.　　Class F.　37 Cents.

MODE

Ten Line Border No. 42.　$2.00 per foot, complete for two colors.　Cut from 4 to 12 Lines Pica.

Printed with WADE'S INKS, from H. D. Wade & Co., 50 Ann St., New York.

56

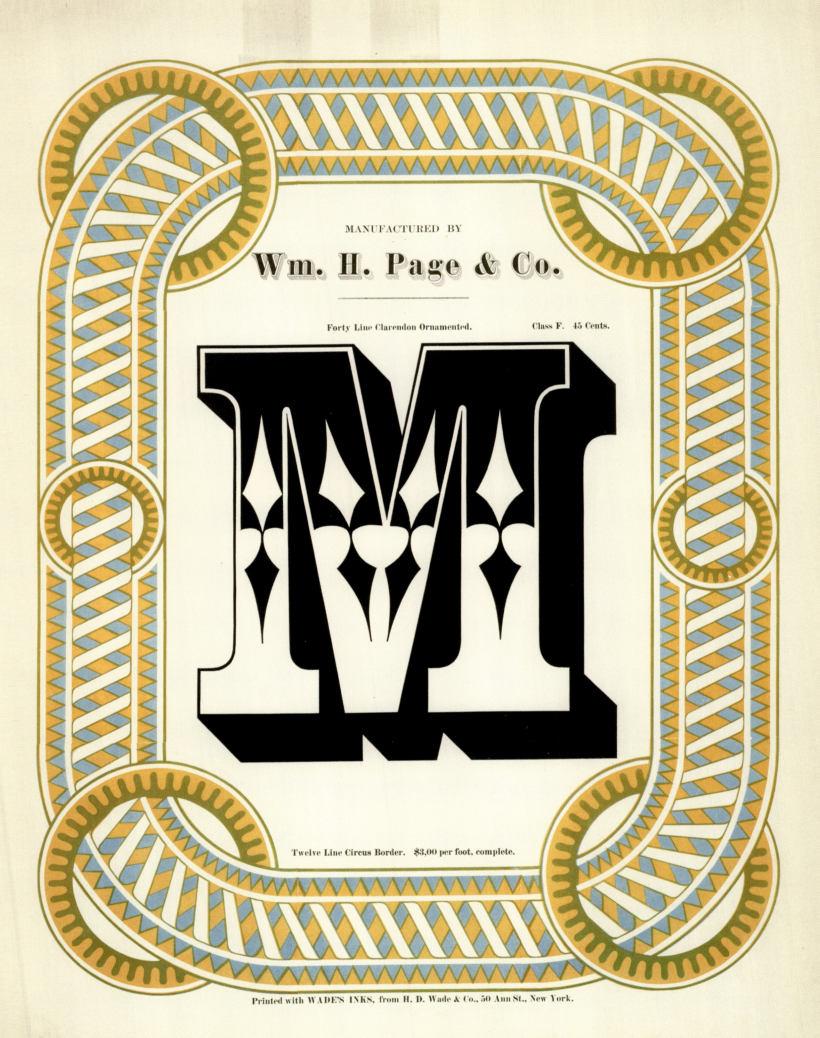

MANUFACTURED BY

Wm. H. Page & Co.

Forty Line Clarendon Ornamented.   Class F.   45 Cents.

Twelve Line Circus Border. $3,00 per foot, complete.

Printed with WADE'S INKS, from H. D. Wade & Co., 50 Ann St., New York.

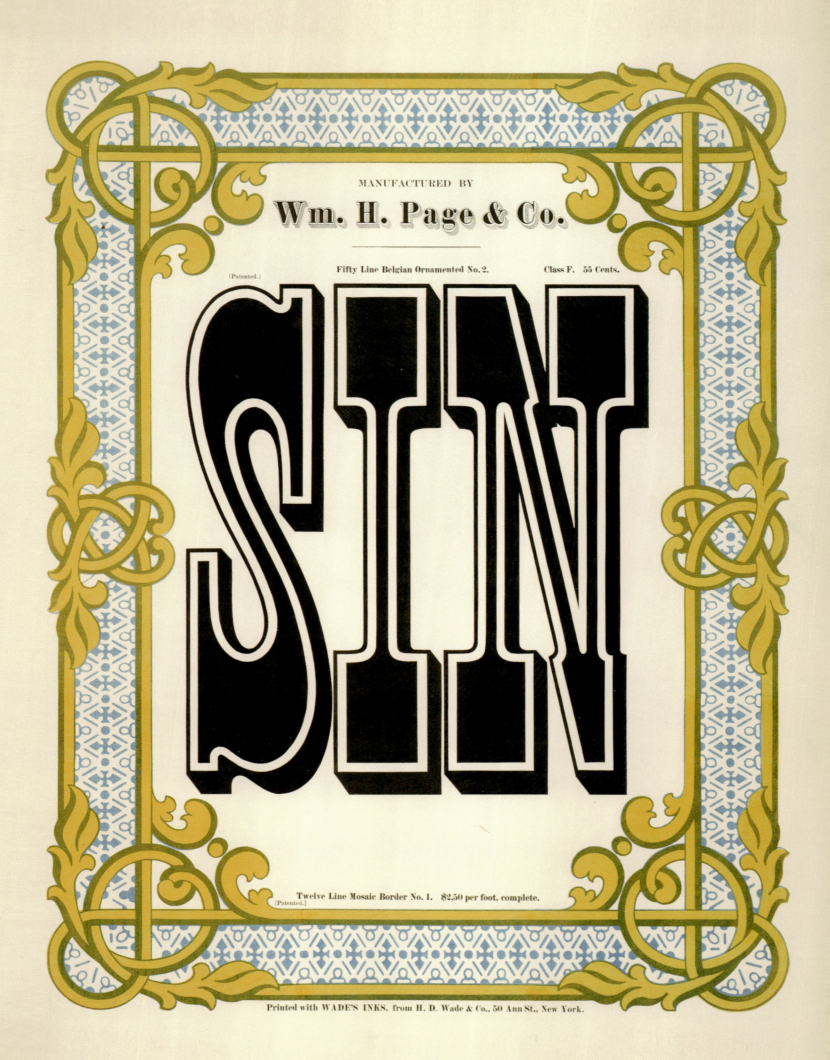

MANUFACTURED BY

Wm. H. Page & Co.

[Patented.]   Fifty Line Belgian Ornamented No. 2.   Class F.   55 Cents.

SIN

Twelve Line Mosaic Border No. 1. $2.50 per foot, complete.
[Patented.]

Printed with WADE'S INKS. from H. D. Wade & Co., 50 Ann St., New York.

Wm. H. Page & Co.

Twelve Line Clarendon Ornamented.   Class F. 17 Cents.

MIXED

Sixteen Line Clarendon Ornamented.   Class F. 21 Cents.

BOLD

Twenty Line Clarendon Ornamented.   Class F. 25 Cents.

HUE

Nine Line Chain Border. $3.00 per foot, complete for three colors.

(Patented Aug. 9, 1870.)

Printed with WADE'S INKS, from H. D. Wade & Co., 50 Ann St., New York.

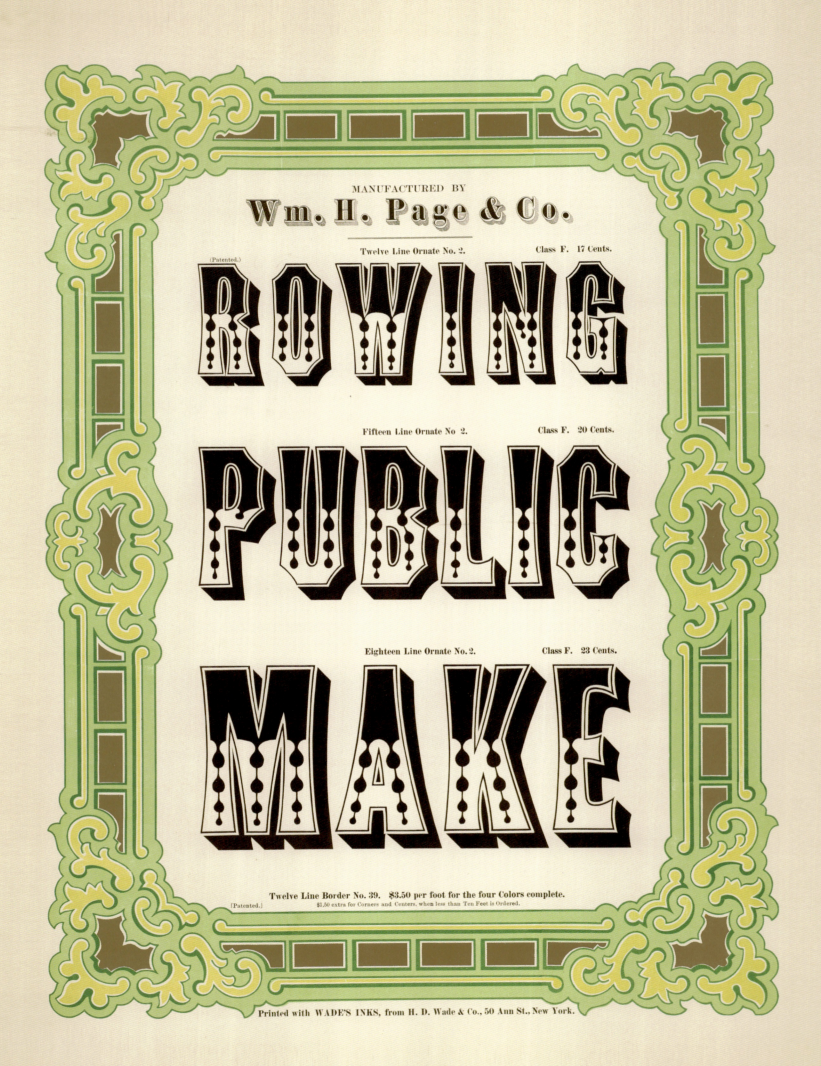

MANUFACTURED BY

Wm. H. Page & Co.

Twelve Line Ornate No. 2.   Class F.   17 Cents.

(Patented.)

ROWING

Fifteen Line Ornate No 2.   Class F.   20 Cents.

PUBLIC

Eighteen Line Ornate No. 2.   Class F.   23 Cents.

MAKE

Twelve Line Border No. 39. $3.50 per foot for the four Colors complete.
[Patented.] $1.50 extra for Corners and Centers, when less than Ten Feet is Ordered.

Printed with WADE'S INKS, from H. D. Wade & Co., 50 Ann St., New York.

60